Entrepreneur Magazine's

Consulting Business

Entrepreneur Magazine's **start-ups**

Consulting Business

John Riddle

Entrepreneur
Press

Managing Editor: Marla Markman
Cover Design: Dunn and Associates
Composition and production: Eliot House Productions

This publication is designed to provide accurate and authoritative information in
regard to the subject matter covered. It is sold with the understanding that the publisher is not engaged in rendering legal, accounting, or other professional services.
If legal advice or other expert assistance is required, the services of a competent
professional person should be sought.

Library of Congress Cataloging-in-Publication Data

Riddle, John.
    Entrepreneur magazine's start-ups : consulting business / John Riddle
       p. cm.
    Includes index.
    ISBN 1-891984-27-6
     1. Business consultants. 2 Career changes. 3. Entrepreneurship. 4. New business
enterprises--Management. I. Title: Start-ups. II. Entrepreneur (Santa Monica, Calif.)
III. Title.

    HD69.C6 R535 2001
    001'.068--dc21   2001023243

Printed in Canada

09 08 07 06 05 04 03 02 01   10 9 8 7 6 5 4 3 2 1

Contents

chapter 1

The Right Stuff

The dictionary defines a consultant as "an expert in a particular field who works as an advisor either to a company or to another individual." Sounds pretty vague, doesn't it? But unless you've been in a coma for the past decade, you probably have a good idea what a consultant is.

Businesses certainly understand what consultants are. In 1997 U.S. businesses spent just over $12 billion on consulting. According to Anna Flowers, spokesperson for the Association of Professional Consultants in Irvine, California, the association has recently noticed an increase in calls for information from people who want to get into the business. "The market is opening up for [the consulting-for-businesses] arena," Flowers says.

Melinda P., an independent consultant in Arlington, Virginia, thinks more people are getting into the consulting field because technology has made it easier to do so. "The same technology that has helped me to be successful as a consultant has made it easier for others to do the same," she says.

A consultant's job is to consult. Nothing more, nothing less. It's that simple. There is no magic formula or secret that makes one consultant more successful than another one.

But what separates a good consultant from a bad consultant is a passion and drive for excellence. And—oh yes—a good consultant should be knowledgeable about the subject he or she is consulting in. That *does* make a difference.

You see, in this day and age, anyone can be a consultant. All you need to discover is what your particular gift is. For example, are you very comfortable working around computers? Do you keep up with the latest software and hardware information, which seems to be changing almost daily? And are you able to take that knowledge you have gained and turn it into a resource that someone would be willing to pay money for? Then you would have no trouble working as a computer consultant.

Or are you an expert in the fund-raising field? Maybe you have worked for non-profit agencies in fund-raising, marketing, public relations, or sales, and over the years you have discovered how to raise money. As someone who has turned a decade of fund-raising successes into a lucrative consulting business, I can tell you that fund-raising consulting is indeed a growing industry.

Fund-raising is growing in small social services agencies, such as soup kitchens and homeless shelters, and in large universities, colleges, and nonprofit hospitals. Once you have successfully learned how to write grant proposals to foundations and corporations and get a few years of experience under your belt, there's no reason you shouldn't be joining the ranks of fund-raising consultants who are earning six figures—and more.

And in case you are wondering, yes, it is possible to be a consultant in more than one

Smart Tip

Before you decide on a consulting specialty, make sure you have a passion for that field. If you can imagine talking with someone for hours at a time about your specialty without referring to notes or books, then you clearly have selected the right field in which to work as a consultant.

field at the same time. You see, in addition to having built a successful fund-raising consulting business, I was simultaneously using my gift of writing to develop an editorial consulting business. It wasn't unusual to find myself meeting with the board of directors of a nonprofit agency concerning fund-raising strategies one day, and the next day showing a client how to break into the publishing world by writing book reviews for his or her local newspaper. I must confess, however, that at times I wished I had concentrated on one or the other field and not felt so compelled to work in different areas.

Beware!

If you decide to do consulting in more than one field, be certain that you can devote enough time and energy to both; otherwise, you run the risk of having both of your consulting specialties fail.

When it comes right down to it, working as a consultant can be a very exciting and lucrative opportunity. Where else can you work as a self-employed, independent agent, set your own hours, and even set your own fees? Of course, you must be willing to devote the time and effort it takes to make a living as a consultant; otherwise, your consulting business will be doomed to fail even before it gets off the ground.

The three most important words all consultants must learn and remember are: marketing, marketing, and marketing. And did I mention marketing? *That's* how important marketing is to all kinds of consultants. You see, if you're not comfortable with marketing and selling your services as a consultant, then you are faced with the choice of either hiring someone to do your marketing for you or learning how to do it yourself. We'll cover both of those scenarios in Chapter 4. But for now, remember that nursery rhyme that you learned as a child: To market, to market, to buy a fat pig... I won't bore you with the rest of the words, but the point is, if you are not ready to market yourself and your consulting services, you will never be able to buy a skinny pig, let alone a fat one. But don't worry. Marketing doesn't have to be scary. Trust me. When I first began working as a consultant, I confess that I wasn't exactly jumping for joy at the prospect of knocking on doors and, in essence, saying, "Hey, wanna pay me big bucks to tell you what to do?"

There are tricks of the trade that you will learn about in Chapter 4, which is devoted to marketing.

Before You Become a Consultant

1. What certifications and special licensing will I need? Depending upon your profession, you may need special certification or a special license before you can begin

Five Good Reasons to Become a Consultant

Although money is sometimes a key factor when someone decides to become a consultant, there are a few other reasons why people choose this profession:

1. You are not living your dream. Maybe your dream has been to work on your own, to be your own boss. As a consultant, you are responsible for your career, not someone else.

2. You are about to lose your job (or have already lost your job). Job security is almost a thing of the past, as everyone knows. Gone are the days when you work for the same company for 20 or 30 years, receive your gold watch, and spend your retirement fishing. As a consultant, you have the power to control your economic future—and ultimate happiness.

3. You have a talent people will pay money for. Suppose that for 20 years you learned how to raise money for nonprofit organizations, and during that time period you built quite a reputation for yourself. Odds are, people will pay you for your talent. (I should know; it happened to me.)

4. You want an additional source of income. Maybe your goal or desire is to only work part time as a consultant. Many consultants in this country are successfully supplementing their incomes by practicing on the side. Be advised, however, if your consulting business begins to interfere with your main job, you may have to choose between the two.

5. You believe you can make a difference. Many people become consultants simply because they know they can do a particular job better than someone else. If you believe in something, nothing should stand in your way.

operating as a consultant. For example, fund-raising consultants don't need special certification, although you can become certified through the National Society of Fund-Raising Executives. And in some states, you may need to register as a professional fund-raising consultant before starting your business.

2. Am I qualified to become a consultant? Before you hang out your shingle and hope that clients begin beating your door down to hire you, make sure you have the qualifications necessary to get the job done. If you want to be a computer consultant, for example, make sure you are up to date in the knowledge department with all the trends and changes in the computer industry.

3. Am I organized enough to become a consultant? Do I like to plan my day? Am I an expert when it comes to time management? You should have answered "yes" to all three of those questions.

4. Do I like to network? Networking is critical to the success of any type of consultant today. Begin building your network of contacts immediately.

5. Have I set long-term and short-term goals? And do they allow for me to become a consultant? If your goals do not match up with the time and energy it takes to open and successfully build a consulting business, then reconsider before making any move in this direction.

> **Bright Idea**
>
> Develop your own short-term and long-term goals, and put them down on paper. Revise them as often as necessary. By having your goals written down, you will be more likely to meet them.

What Exactly Do Consultants Do, Anyway?

While many people have a preconceived notion of what a consultant looks like and actually does, the truth is, consultants are just regular people. While you may have to work harder to become successful as a consultant, there are some important skills you need to succeed:

○ *Listening skills:* When people talk, do you listen? This may sound like a dumb question, but listening is an acquired skill. By carefully listening to your clients' needs, you will be able to solve their problems.

○ *Investigative skills:* You need to have the ability to investigate and uncover the data necessary to complete your consulting assignment. In time, your investigative skills will become fine-tuned.

○ *Analytical skills:* When you investigate and uncover data, you had better know what it means. Your ability to understand and analyze complex information relative to your consulting field of expertise is paramount.

○ *Change skills:* No, we don't mean exact change for the bus. But you must be a person who *embraces* change and who can convince your client to make the changes necessary to solve his or her problem.

○ *Action skills:* A good consultant will be ready to "take the bull by the horns" and

> **Smart Tip**
>
> How good a listener are you? The next time you are having a conversation with someone, resist the urge to interrupt with questions or your own comments until they have completely finished what they are saying.

do whatever it takes to get the job done. In other words, you will take action with a capital "A."

A Brief History of Consulting

It wasn't until the 1950s that consultants began to emerge in the business world. Until then, consultants could be found in the legal, finance, and employment fields. Then something happened. When the United States economy changed from a production-oriented one to a service-oriented one in the early 1960s, the real birth of the consulting industry took place. Since most consultants were providing a service as an expert in a particular field, they were welcomed with open arms by both large and small businesses throughout the land.

Then, during the economic recession of the late 1970s and early 1980s, corporate America suddenly found it difficult to turn a profit. There seemed to be no other way to boost the bottom line other than reducing staff. So, little by little, businesses began to cut back on operating costs by offering early retirement packages to long-term employees and laying off anyone they felt was expendable.

From a corporate point of view, the thinking was simply "It makes sense to hire a consultant," since paying a consultant seemed like a cost-effective means of doing business. So not only was there a boost in the demand for consultants, many people who had accepted early retirement packages were now setting up shop as consultants. And many people found themselves working as consultants to the very businesses that had let them go or had forced them into early retirement.

At the same time, many consultants were faced with a dilemma most people never have to face: *too much business*. So rather than turn away a client, many independent consultants joined with other consultants in their field, and thus, the birth of the consulting industry took place.

According to a recent survey, these are the top ten reasons organizations hire consultants:

1. A consultant may be hired because of his or her expertise. This is where it pays to not only be really good in the field you have chosen to consult in, but to have some type of track record that speaks for itself. For example, when I mentioned earlier that I had become an expert as a fund-raising consultant, I knew that every client who hired me was doing so partly on the basis of my track record. After all, if you are a nonprofit organization that needs to raise $1 million, it makes sense to hire someone who has already raised millions for other organizations.

2. A consultant may be hired to identify problems. Sometimes employees are too close to a problem inside an organization to identify it. That's when a consultant rides in on his or her white horse to save the day.

3. A consultant may be hired to supplement the staff. Sometimes a business discovers that it can save thousands of dollars a week by hiring consultants when they are needed, rather than hiring full-time employees. Businesses realize they save additional money by not having to pay benefits for consultants they hire. Even though a consultant's fees are generally higher than an employee's salary, over the long haul, it simply makes good economic sense to hire a consultant.

4. A consultant may be hired to act as a catalyst. Let's face it. No one likes change, especially corporate America. But sometimes change is needed, and a consultant may be brought in to "get the ball rolling." In other words, the consultant can do things without worrying about the corporate culture, employee morale, or other issues that get in the way when an organization is trying to institute change.

5. A consultant may be hired to provide much-needed objectivity. Who else is more qualified to identify a problem than a consultant? A good consultant provides an objective, fresh viewpoint—without worrying about what people in the organization might think about the results of changes they make and how they were achieved.

6. A consultant may be hired to teach. These days if you are a computer consultant who can show employees how to master a new program, then your telephone probably hasn't stopped ringing for a while. A consultant may be asked to teach employees any number of different skills. However, a consultant must be willing to keep up with new discoveries in their field of expertise—and be ready to teach new clients what they need to stay competitive.

7. A consultant may be hired to do the "dirty work." Let's face it: no one wants to be the person who has to make cuts in the staff or eliminate an entire division.

8. A consultant may be hired to bring new life to an organization. If you are good at coming up with new ideas that work, then you won't have any trouble finding clients. At one time or another, most businesses need someone to administer "first aid" to get things rolling again.

9. A consultant may be hired to create a new business. There are consultants who have become experts in this field. Not everyone, though, has the ability to conceive an idea and develop a game plan.

10. A consultant may be hired to influence other people. Do you like to hang out with the rich and famous in your town? If so, you may be hired to do a consulting job simply based on who you know. Although most consultants in this field are working as lobbyists, there has been an increase in the number of people entering the entertainment consulting business.

> **Beware!**
> Before accepting any consulting assignment, be certain that the potential client is not involved in any litigation concerning employment discrimination practices.

Top 20 Consulting Businesses Thriving Today

Although you can be a consultant in just about any field these days, the top 20 consulting businesses thriving today include:

1. *Accounting*. Let's face it: Accounting is something that every business needs, no matter how large or small. Accounting consultants can help a business with all of its financial needs.

2. *Advertising*. With the price of advertising these days, it's no wonder that anyone with any type of advertising expertise can earn a good living as an advertising consultant. (This type of consultant is normally hired by a business to develop a good strategic advertising campaign.)

3. *Auditing*. From consultants who audit utility bills for small businesses to consultants who handle major work for telecommunications firms, auditing consultants are enjoying the fruits of their labor. (This type of consultant is normally hired to audit various utility bills for corporations.)

4. *Business*. Know how to help a business turn a profit? If you have a good business sense, then you'll do well as a business consultant. After computer consulting, people in this field are the next most sought after.

5. *Business writing*. Everyone knows that most businesspeople have trouble when it comes to writing a report—or even a simple memo. Enter the business writing consultant, and everyone is happy.

6. *Career counseling*. With more and more people finding themselves victims of a corporate downsizing, career counselors will always be in demand. Career counselors guide their clients into a profession or job that will help them be both happy and productive as an employee.

7. *Communications*. A good communications consultant will never have to worry about where her next meal is coming from. Communications consultants specialize in helping employees in both large and small businesses better communicate with each other, which ultimately makes the business more efficient and operate smoothly.

8. *Computer consulting*. From software to hardware, and everything in between, if you know computers, your biggest

> **Bright Idea**
> Develop your own top ten list. Make a list of the top ten reasons why a business should hire you as a consultant. This will help you when you prepare your marketing strategy.

'Tis the Reason

Before you decide to open up your own shop, think carefully about why you want to become a consultant. It's important that you don't become a consultant for all the wrong reasons. For example, if you and your boss are not getting along, but you have had your differences with him or her in the past—and always reached an understanding—then you probably don't want to leave your job and become a consultant. However, if you are really dissatisfied with your boss and your company, and can envision doing the work more efficiently on your own, then you are probably doing it for all the right reasons.

problem will be not having enough hours in the day to meet your clients' demands.

9. *Editorial services.* From producing newsletters to corporate annual reports, consultants who are experts in the editorial field will always be appreciated.

10. *Executive search/headhunter firms.* While this is not for everyone, there are people who enjoy finding talent for employers.

11. *Gardening.* In the past decade the demand for gardening consultants has blossomed (pun intended) into a $1 million-a-year business. Not only are businesses hiring gardening consultants; so are people who are too busy to take care of their gardens at home.

12. *Grantsmanship.* Once you learn how to write a grant proposal, you can name your price.

13. *Human resources.* As long as businesses have people problems (and they always will), consultants in this field will enjoy a never-ending supply of corporate clients, both large and small. (People-problem prevention programs could include teaching employees to get along with others, teaching employees to respect and get along with others.)

14. *Insurance.* Everyone needs insurance, and everyone needs an insurance consultant to help them find the best plan and pricing for them.

15. *Marketing.* Can you help a business write a marketing plan? Or do you have ideas that you feel will help promote a business? If so, why not try your hand as a marketing consultant?

16. *Payroll management.* Everyone needs to get paid. By using your knowledge and expertise in payroll management, you can provide this service to many businesses, both large and small.

17. *Public relations.* Getting good press coverage for any organization is a real art. When an organization finds a good PR consultant, they hang on to them for life.

18. *Publishing.* If you are interested in the publishing field, then learn everything you can and you, too, can be a publishing consultant. A publishing consultant usually helps new ventures when they are ready to launch a newspaper, magazine, newsletter—and even Web sites and electronic newsletters.

19. *Taxes.* With the right marketing and business plan (and a sincere interest in taxes), your career as a tax consultant can be very lucrative. A tax consultant advises businesses on the legal methods to pay the least amount of tax possible.

20. *Writing services.* Anything related to the written word will always be in demand. Find your specialty in the writing field, and the sky will be the limit.

chapter 2

Finding Your Specialty

To be a really successful consultant, you need to be working in a field in which you are an expert. You see, working as a consultant is different than going to work as an employee. Every day in this country, millions of people go to work. Most of them are probably not happy with their jobs for one reason or another. It may be due to low pay, a long commute, or maybe they just don't get along with their boss. It doesn't matter why they are unhappy; they just are.

I confess that more than 20 years ago I was one of those people. I went to work every day, hated my job, despised the corporate culture, and was generally not a happy camper. At the time, I was working in the payroll department of a large chemical company in Delaware. Although I was good at the job I was doing, my true passion was not handling the payroll and the endless reports we had to produce.

Bright Idea

Do you have a hobby that you might be able to turn into a successful consulting business? If you collect antiques, for example, you may be able to use your knowledge of the antiques industry to provide appraisal services.

Instead, my true passion was writing. And even though I had no real experience as a writer, I had read nearly every book that had been written about how to make it as a writer. So after seven years in the payroll department, I left the company and went to work for a small public relations firm, where I was able to do some promotional writing and event planning.

It didn't matter that I had taken a pay cut, or that job security was no longer a benefit. I was working in my true passion area. I was a writer. And within a few years I had written several books and started selling newspaper and magazine articles to publications throughout the country. I had found happiness and contentment, all because I was doing something that I truly enjoyed. It was no longer "Thank God It's Friday," but "Thank God It's Monday."

So do you know what your field of expertise is? What subject can you talk about for hours at a time without worrying about how long you have been talking? Now don't confuse something you do in your spare time—like, for example, being an avid soap opera fan—with a field of expertise. Yes, you truly are concerned about Luke and Laura on "General Hospital." But unless you are going to turn that interest into some type of consulting business, you need to re-examine where your true priorities lie.

Beware!

Be certain that there is a market for your chosen consulting field. If you choose a specialty so obscure that you have no clients, then obviously you will have no business.

As I mentioned earlier, I discovered that one of my true passions is writing. Not only have I been published in a variety of media over the past 20 years; I have also taught workshops and published newsletters to show people how to break into the wonderful world of freelance writing. When I present my workshops, it's not unusual for me to end up staying an hour or so afterwards just to answer questions or to help someone who is not quite sure if they understand what they need to do to become a freelance writer.

I also keep in touch with students who have attended my workshops. In fact, the first thing I do in the opening session is write my home telephone number on the blackboard. Then I tell everyone that they should copy that number down somewhere. And much to everyone's surprise, I offer to answer questions anytime in the future. All they have to do is call me.

I tell them not only is it OK to call and ask questions or seek advice on how to get published, but if they have a success and want to share the good news with someone, I'm there for them. You see, I remind them that at one

> ## Smart Tip
> Since the consulting business is all about people, use every opportunity available to develop a relationship with the people you are working for. Be someone they will come to depend on now and in the future.

time, I had never been published, but I kept trying and never gave up. I know what it's like to get that first article published in a newspaper or a magazine and be busting out all over with happiness. But maybe your parents, spouse, significant other, or even your co-workers don't share your enthusiasm. That's where I come in. Call me, I tell them. Let me share in your good news; after all, I've been there, done that.

And yes, over the years, my former students have called me to share both rejections *and* success stories. There have even been a few people who ended up hiring me as their personal editorial consultant. You see, they wanted to learn from someone who had broken into the publishing industry and become an expert in that field. In other words, they were willing to pay me, on average, $65 per hour to tell them what to do.

Assessing Your Skills and Talents

People who want a career as a consultant should be aware of both their strengths *and* weaknesses and how relevant they are to this type of work if they are to be effective in their role. For example, if your writing skills leave much to be desired, then you will have a difficult time preparing reports for your clients.

You also need to be prepared to talk about your business—all of the time and to everybody you meet. That philosophy has helped Roxanne W., a consultant in Wilmington, Delaware. "Never shut up. Never be quiet. Talk to everybody and anybody you come into contact with. Let everyone know what you are doing and when you are doing it," she says.

While some people may already know—or *think* they know—what type of consulting field they want to break into, it really is a good idea to take some time to assess your skills and talents. Remember how I said I had worked in the payroll department for seven years—but wasn't really happy? Well, even though I did not like my job, I was good at what I had to accomplish each day. And like any other job, it got easier—and I learned how to do it better as time passed.

I was skilled and talented in the area of payroll and finances. The difference between happiness in what you do is simply the difference between your skills and talents and your true passion. We'll talk more about how to find your true passion in just a bit—and how you can turn that passion into a lucrative consulting business. But first, let's talk briefly about how to discover your skills and talents.

For years, career counseling consultants have been advising their clients to make a list of what they feel they excel at and compare that to a list of things they would rather spend their day doing. Sometimes people have talents in areas they weren't ever aware of. For example, a young mother who has made the decision to stay at home with her children has had to master the fine arts of time management (scheduling time for her, the children, and her husband), budgeting (paying bills, banking, and money management), and even negotiation (ever try to get two children to agree with each other? It's not easy.).

Take a look at the work sheet on page 15. After you have answered those questions, make a list of the things you can do (with regards to your potential consulting career). At the same time, make a list of things that you would rather be doing. Remember, there are no right or wrong answers.

Your list might look something like mine:

Things I can do: typing, special event planning, teaching, researching, writing, editing, sales, public relations, and promotions.

Things I would rather be doing: collecting big, fat royalty checks, writing, dancing, teaching writing workshops, watching television, and going to the movies.

So how did I stack up? Did I look fairly normal? You see, it should come as no surprise to many people that some items will appear on both lists. And when you come across items that appear on both lists, then you have discovered one way of finding out where your true interests lie. In other words, your true passion areas will determine how successful a consultant you become.

Writing, teaching writing workshops, and event planning are three areas I have been excelling in over the past few years. So it should come as no surprise to everyone that my career choices have been leaning in those directions. As I look back over my years of employment, I

Beware!
When putting together your list of what you do well, think back to years past. Perhaps you have a talent you have not used in many years that may still be something to consider when starting your consulting business.

Skills and Talents Work Sheet

If you don't acknowledge your hidden skills and talents, you will never be able to present them to your clients—and make a living at the same time.

So grab a pencil, and get ready to work.

○ What job skills do you possess that are really outstanding?

_____

_____

_____

○ What specialized training or education do you have?

_____

_____

_____

○ What do you like the most about your present job or occupation?

_____

_____

_____

○ What special license(s) do you possess in your present job?

_____

_____

_____

○ What have you been told that you do extremely well?

_____

_____

_____

have been the happiest—and most productive—in jobs that have made use of my true skills and talents.

So as you prepare to launch your consulting career, don't forget to do some real soul searching and select a field in which you will really excel.

Could You Teach a Workshop in Your Field of Expertise?

One surefire way to discover if the field you have chosen is one that you will be successful in is to put together enough material to teach a workshop. (We'll talk more about how a workshop can increase your cash flow and enhance your bottom line in Chapter 5.) It doesn't have to be anything fancy—just a workshop that will hold people's attention and give them some good information about the subject you are teaching.

Let me share a brief story with you about how I came to discover that I was very good at presenting workshops. I had no real teaching experience but felt compelled to share my experiences as a freelance writer with other people who were trying to break into that field. You see, I had struggled for nearly five years without successfully publishing anything. Even though I had been reading every book I could find on the subject, and had even attended a few workshops for beginning writers myself, I was still not having any luck getting published.

Then one day I read an article in *Writer's Digest* magazine about how newspapers and magazines were always on the lookout for freelance writers to write book reviews. The article took me step-by-step through the process of getting my first book review published. And much to my surprise, the advice *worked*. Within a few weeks of reading that article (which I now use as a handout in my writing workshops), my first book review was published.

Ten Qualities Good Consultants Possess

1. Intelligence
2. Flexibility
3. Critical thinking skills
4. Reliability
5. Excellent communication skills
6. Resourcefulness
7. Integrity
8. Perseverance
9. Sense of humor
10. Dedication

That book review with my byline opened up so many publishing opportunities for me that it was unbelievable. You see, in the world of writing and publishing, one clip (a copy of an article you have written) is worth its weight in gold.

So about five years ago I decided to offer a workshop for beginning freelance writers. I called it "Introduction to Freelance Writing" and contacted a local school district to see if it was interested in including my workshop in its fall catalog of noncredit courses it was offering to adults in the evening hours. They were delighted and asked me to submit a course description the next day.

Writing the course description was not a problem. In fact, this is what I came up with:

> *Writing is an act of courage! Discipline, creativity, boldness, and determination are mixed up in it too, but writing is above all an act of courage. Writers must possess the courage to believe that what they have said is worthy of being read by others. Walt Disney once said, "If you can dream it, you can do it." If you have ever dreamed of seeing your name on a byline in a newspaper or magazine article but didn't know how to achieve that goal, then this course is for you. Here you will learn how to get started as a freelance writer. Instructional materials and handouts will help you stop collecting rejection slips and begin collecting checks. At the end of this course, you will know how to get published.*

After the course catalog had been in circulation for only one week, I received a telephone call from a school district representative who informed me that my workshop was full and that they were looking forward to having it begin in just three short weeks. When we hung up, I was both happy and worried. I was happy because now I was going to be able to teach a course for beginning freelance writers, but I was worried because I had no idea what I was going to actually teach.

But I was pretty sure that I would be able to put something together in no time at all. Besides, I told myself, this is a ten-week course, so I'll just play it by ear and see how each week goes. In retrospect, this was both a plus and a minus. On one hand, I was able to see what the skill level of the workshop participants was before I decided what material to present each week. But on the other hand, everyone kept asking for a course outline, because they were anxious to find out what they would be learning during the ten weeks.

So after carefully reviewing my files (which were filled with nearly 20 years' worth of writing advice), I came up with a course outline and found out that I had more material than I could ever use. The point I am trying to make here is this: if you are both passionate and knowledgeable about your chosen consulting field, you should be able and willing to present a workshop on it.

Who Is Your Target Audience?

Your idea may be the best one you have ever thought of, but there needs to be a market for your ideas. In other words, someone must be willing and able to pay you for your expert advice.

Now we are going to get serious about your chosen consulting field. By now you have learned that you need to be excited, interested, passionate, and an expert in whatever it is you have chosen to consult about. But there is one more very important feature to consider: Just who is your target audience?

In other words, who are your potential clients? Will you be marketing your consulting services to large corporations? Or will you offer a specialty that would only be of interest to smaller businesses? Perhaps your services will be sought after by nonprofit organizations. Whatever the case, before you go forward, make sure you spend time preparing both a business plan and a marketing plan. You won't be disappointed with the results—especially when clients begin paying you.

Smart Tip

Tip

Take a few minutes and brainstorm as to who you think your first ten clients would be. Is this list easy for you to develop? If so, you have the right attitude. If the list is difficult to produce, rethink why you are getting into the consulting business.

Can You Make a Difference?

Before you climb that ladder and prepare to take the plunge into the wonderful world of consulting, be sure that what you are offering to do for a client will make a difference for them. If you're not sure if you can make a difference, ask yourself these five questions:

1. Am I confident that I can solve a client's problem?

2. Am I confident that I can find new and creative solutions to these problems?

3. Am I confident that I can meet the deadlines and work in almost any environment?

4. Am I confident that I can work within the budget presented by the client?

5. Am I confident that I can repeat steps one through four every day?

Outstanding in the Field

If you want to start earning in the six-figure range, you need to become an outstanding consultant, not a mediocre one. And the basic difference between the two can be narrowed down to a simple top ten list:

1. *Eat, drink, and breathe customer service.* If you do not live by the creed of "giving more than you have," you won't be remembered as a consultant who goes the extra mile for customers.

2. *Keep up with the latest changes in your field of expertise.* Read professional journals, attend workshops, and network with other people in your field.

3. *Develop the ability to identify problems quickly.* Know what you're talking about. Clients hire you because of your expertise; don't disappoint them.

4. *Look for creative ways to solve problems.* Put your thinking cap on.

5. *Use excellent communication skills.* Enhance your communication skills. Read, attend workshops, practice writing reports—whatever it takes.

6. *Be 100 percent confident that you will succeed.* Everyone likes to work with someone who can prove that everything they undertake will be a success.

7. *Be professional in everything you do.* (This had better not warrant further explanation; otherwise you might want to reconsider your decision to get into the consulting business.)

8. *Be a people person.* It takes a real "people person" to be a successful consultant. How are your people skills?

9. *Be the best manager you can be.* Be ready, willing, and able to be the best manager you can be. Good managers are expert at time management and doing whatever it takes to get the job done.

10. *Give your clients more than they expect.* Give clients more than they ask for. You'll be surprised at their responses.

Defining Your Market

Who are the people who will pay you for your services? Remember that in the world of the consulting business, it's not who you know or even who you have worked for in the past that is important to potential clients. The main question every potential client will be asking is "What can you do for *me?*"

A few years ago, I almost lost a consulting client. A local nonprofit theater group was looking for a fund-raising consultant to design a plan and raise a little more than

Getting Friendly with the Internet

The Internet can be a consultant's best friend. Once you become Internet-savvy, you will discover the multitude of information in cyberspace which will help you as you grow and expand your consulting practice. Check out some of these Web sites:

○ *Consultant's Corner* <www.pwgroup.com/corner>: Consultant's Corner is an excellent source for listings of consultants, training and resource materials, small-business survival guides and much more.

○ *Association of Professional Consultants* <www.consultapc.org>: This is an excellent resource for consultants in all fields. Information can be found on publicity and promotions, professional workshops and courses, and a whole plethora of business subjects of interest to consulting professionals.

○ *Expert Marketplace* <www.expert-market.com/em>: This unique Web site contains listings of more than 200,000 consulting firms and individuals. With its searchable database, you will have no trouble finding consultants you can network with in locations around the country.

○ *The Small Business Administration* <www.sba.gov>: The SBA is an excellent online resource for consultants who are just starting out in their own practice. Everything from advice on promoting your business to financial planning is available with the click of your mouse.¡¡

---

half-a-million dollars so they could make some improvements to their building. They had narrowed their search down to another consultant and myself. Because we were probably equally qualified, it was difficult for them to choose one over another. So they called us both back in for a few more interview questions. I arrived early and sat outside the boardroom waiting patiently for my turn.

Much to my surprise, I was able to hear what was taking place inside that room. The other candidate was busy talking about what contacts he had made in the entertainment industry, including the theatrical world. He was dropping names that were no doubt impressing the search committee.

Well, right then and there I knew I had two choices. Number one, I could come up with my own list of celebrity contacts (I had done a fair share of celebrity interviews as a freelance writer) and try and dazzle the search committee. Or my second choice was to simply reiterate what I could do for them: I could raise the money they needed within the time frame they had come up with. Period. Nothing more, nothing less.

Guess who got the job?

So in answer to our question "Who are the people who will pay for your services?" the answer is simply this: anyone who has a need you can fill.

Figuring out who you will be trying to solicit as clients doesn't involve a complicated formula. In other words, seek out potential clients in your chosen field of expertise. For example, if you decide to become a fund-raising consultant, check to see what nonprofit organizations in your town need to raise money but don't know how to go about putting a fund-raising plan into action. For more information on market research, check out Chapter 2 of Entrepreneur's *Start-Up Basics*.

Finding Those Clients

Because we will cover this subject in Chapter 4, we don't want to spend too much time talking about how you go about finding potential clients right here.

Dollar Stretcher

There are plenty of free resources available to help you create a list of potential clients: the phone book, the local chamber of commerce directory, the daily newspaper, a network of friends, etc.

chapter 3

Setting Up Shop

This chapter will cover where to locate your business (being homebased is usually a great choice for a consultant), whether or not you need a toll-free number and a Web site, naming your business, and nuts and bolts (like a business license) you may need to run your enterprise.

Your consulting business will probably not require a large capital investment at first. In fact, if you are able to, you should consider operating out of your home. (Certain deed restrictions and local laws may prohibit you from doing this; check with an attorney before you proceed.)

There are many advantages to having a home office. Among them are:

> **Bright Idea**
> Check with your local civic association to see if they have any objection to you operating a service business from your home. It is better to make friends with them *before* you run into any problems.

○ Low overhead expenses. You don't have to worry about paying rent or utilities for an office; you will appreciate this feature until you establish a regular client base.

○ Flexibility. There is little doubt that operating as a consultant at home gives you a great deal of flexibility. You can set your own hours and take time off as you need it.

○ No rush-hour nightmares. For anyone who has had to commute to and from a job during rush hour, this will be a welcome change of pace.

○ Your home office space will most likely be tax-deductible. The IRS has relaxed the rules for people who work at home, but check with your accountant or income tax preparer to see if you qualify for this deduction.

For more information on location, check out Chapter 8 of Entrepreneur's *Start-Up Basics*.

Toll-Free Telephone Numbers, Web Pages, and Other Myths of Success

> **Dollar Stretcher**
> If you want to have your own Web site, try getting one of the free pages available on the Internet (Tripod and Angelfire, just to name a few). Check with your local Internet service provider to see if you get any free Web space as part of your monthly contract.

Before you go broke getting your own toll-free number and paying someone to design a Web site for you, examine carefully your need, or your perceived need, of those items.

As someone who has had both a toll-free number and a page on the Web, I can tell you that you can succeed with or without those luxuries. The determining factor, of course, is how successful you wish to become.

Home Court Disadvantages

Of course, running a business from your home isn't all fun and games. There are a few disadvantages to operating out of your home. These include:

○ Loneliness. If you are used to working in a large office setting with plenty of people, you may be in for a culture shock when you first open your consulting business at home. Make sure you develop a network of friends and other associates to talk with on a regular basis.

○ You may be tempted to do all of those "home" things. It takes a well-disciplined person to work at home. You must be able to say to yourself "I am at work. I will not stop and do the laundry, mow the lawn, shovel snow (or whatever other chore happens to be staring you in the face)."

○ You may have to overcome the stigma of owning "just another homebased business." Some potential clients may not hire you because you don't have an office downtown. But since the number of homebased businesses has been growing over the past decade, and those businesses have been earning the respect they are due, this is becoming less of a disadvantage.

○ Depending on how large or attractive your house is, you may be limited when it comes to seeing clients in your home office.

○ Family members, friends and neighbors may not respect your working time and working space and feel they can interrupt you anytime they want.

Toll-Free Telephone Numbers

Depending on who your target market is, a toll-free number may be just another deductible expense on your income tax return. Or it can be the deciding factor in whether or not your consulting business succeeds.

Twenty years ago, only large corporations were able to afford toll-free telephone numbers, and few people expected them to be available for their convenience and use. These days, however, it seems as if every business, no matter what its size, has a toll-free number. Advances in technology have made it possible for nearly everyone to have a toll-free number.

When I was selling ad space in my fund-raising newsletters, I was targeting companies (and other consultants) who provided products and services all across the

United States. And because I had a toll-free number, potential advertisers could call with any questions or to place their ad order. Many times I asked an advertiser why they selected my newsletter to advertise with. More often than not, their reply was "Because you had a toll-free telephone number."

My prices were very competitive, and the circulation was similar to those of many other fund-raising newsletters being published at the time. My only advantage over the competition was the toll-free telephone number.

If you are considering having your own toll-free telephone number, contact more than one company and get competitive bids. And compare the services you will be receiving, too. For more information on toll-free numbers, read Chapter 15 of Entrepreneur's *Start-Up Basics*.

> ### Smart Tip
> *Tip*
>
> Check with your local telephone company to see what toll-free telephone options are available. You might consider subscribing to a voice-mail service so that you will not miss important incoming telephone calls.

Web Pages

While it will eventually make sense for your consulting business to have a site on the Web, don't rush into this venture just for the sake of saying "Yes, I'm on the Internet." With so many sites on the Web today, it will be worth your while to access some of the search engines (Yahoo!, Alta Vista, Excite, etc.) and see what other consultants have done with their Web pages. Spending just a few minutes on the Internet will give you literally thousands of pages to choose from. Which brings up an important point: Who are you trying to reach with your Web page?

Unless the clients you are trying to reach are online, you are wasting your time and money. Remember, having a Web site doesn't guarantee your success. Let me share a story with you about how I test-marketed a Web page.

About a year ago I decided to sell a fund-raising plan I called the "No Go, No Show" campaign. To make a long story short, I had designed several greeting cards that nonprofit organizations all across the country had been successfully using to solicit contributions for their causes. The cards invited potential donors to an imaginary New Year's Eve dinner party. Instead of attending yet another boring rubber chicken affair, the donor had the luxury of making a contribution and staying home instead. The key to the campaign's success was the way humor was used throughout the card and the reply card the donors used when they sent in their checks.

I hired a Web page designer who took my rough drawings and instructions and turned them into an award-winning Web site. The pages were colorful, interesting, and filled with free fund-raising advice people could use by just visiting the site.

I registered the Web site with the appropriate search engines (you can read more about this process in Chapter 18 of Entrepreneur's *Start-Up Basics*) and waited for the money to start rolling in. Each fund-raising plan came complete with sample cards, instructions, and a toll-free number to call, with no limit on how often a customer could call with questions. I had convinced myself that I was the king of customer service.

But although the site was receiving several hundred hits per day, with visitors from all across the United States and even a half-dozen foreign countries, no one placed an order. I had forgotten the most important rule when it comes to marketing via the Internet: My target audience should be online and Internet-savvy. In this case, my target audience for the "No Go, No Show" fundraising plan was small and midsized social service nonprofit organizations, most of which barely had computers, let alone Internet access.

When I realized the problem, I pulled my Web site. So before you spend time and money putting together a Web site for your consulting business, make sure the people you are trying to reach will be on the other end of the keyboard.

> ### Smart Tip
>
> Before you decide to launch a Web site, make sure you have time to update it at least weekly. Visitors will stop coming to your site if they see the same messages, graphics, information, etc. If you don't have the time or expertise to make the changes yourself, hire someone to make them for you.

Naming Your Business

What's in a name? Plenty, especially if you want your business to be successful. When selecting a name for your consulting business, choose carefully. Take a few moments and browse through the Yellow Pages in your local telephone book; this will often give you a few good lessons on what *not* to name your business. Look under "Consultants," and you will see a wide variety of consulting names. From "ABC Consulting" (do they teach you the alphabet?) to "Kite Associates" (do they teach you to make kites, or just fly them?), or my personal favorite, "The Dolphin Consulting Group" (fill in your favorite "Flipper" joke), the names will vary (and some will actually be very funny). But unless your goal is to provide a good laugh or confuse potential clients, then take some time choosing a name before hanging out your shingle for all of the world to see.

One of the entrepreneurs interviewed for this book came up with the name for her consulting business based on the services she provided. Her business is called Adhelp. "I'm actually helping people with their advertising, so I just put the words 'ad' and

When deciding on a name for your consulting business, be sensitive to how that name might translate into another language. For example, if you will be dealing with foreign clients (even in this country), you want to make sure your business name is not offensive when translated into their native language.

'help' together," she says. "And I knew that because it began with the letter 'a,' it would always be listed near the top."

Other entrepreneurs interviewed for this book found the monikers for their businesses right in front of their noses—they used variations of their names and counted on their family's recognition within the community.

I chose Blue Moon Communications as the name of my consulting business. I thought it was a catchy name, and it didn't limit the services I might provide in the future. After all, a communications business would be able to offer a variety of services: consulting, publishing, workshops, etc.

As a consultant, you want to portray an aura of professionalism, so try and stay away from cutesy names. If you aren't sure what to call your business, try something simple like "John Doe and Associates" or even "John Doe, Consultant." Just be sure that when you advertise in the telephone book, you are specific about the type of consulting services you offer. (For example, if you offer management consulting services, be sure you are placed in that category.)

Business Licenses and Other Necessary Paperwork

Make sure you obtain all of the business licenses you need to operate in your community. Just contact the department of licensing in your town and they will tell you what you need. Jeffery B., a consultant in Harrisburg, Pennsylvania, says there is no special license needed for the work his firm performs. "We provide focus group facilities to our clients, and we only need a business license to operate," he says.

In addition to a business license, if you are a consultant in a specialized field, such as accounting, you will probably need to have a license to do business. Check with the appropriate state agency for additional information. For more on business licenses and permits, check out Chapter 5 of Entrepreneur's *Start-Up Basics*.

chapter 4

Finding and Keeping Clients

In this chapter, we will discuss the most important aspect of your consulting business: where to find clients. We'll also look at how to keep those clients once you have found them.

If your consulting business has no clients, then you have no consulting business. But you must remember that selling your consulting services is not the same as selling a car or a house. In the case of the car or the house, the customer is probably already in the market for one or both of those products. Your job, then, becomes harder, because you are marketing your services to people who may not even be aware that they need those services.

There are a variety of methods you need to become both familiar and comfortable with in order to begin attracting and keeping clients. Let's look at some of the more conventional ones that are being used by many consultants today.

Direct Mail

Anyone who is seriously considering starting a consulting business better know at least the basics of direct mail (if you want to learn more about direct mail, there are some excellent books listed in this book's appendix).

With direct mail, you simply send your prospective clients your brochure, a flier, or a letter describing the consulting services you offer. It doesn't take a rocket scientist to come up with an award-winning direct-mail campaign. In fact, if you think about it, *you* are already an expert in the direct-mail field. When you get home from a hard day at the office and the mail is tossed onto the kitchen table or counter, what process do you use to sort through it?

If you are like most people, you pull out the bills, set them aside, then look to see if any personal letters or cards have arrived. Then, and only then, do you begin to look through the junk mail. Now don't get upset, because when it comes right down to it, any direct-mail piece will sooner or later be classified as junk mail. Don't take it personally; it's just a fact of life.

So when you come across an interesting piece of direct mail, you open it to see what exciting offers are hidden inside. What motivated you to open the envelope—even though you knew it was just another attempt to sell you something? You see, in the exciting world of direct mail, getting someone to open the envelope is half the battle. So now you know why businesses, government agencies, nonprofit organizations—virtually anyone with anything to sell via direct mail—invest so much time and expense designing just the right "sell piece." Take a look at the sample direct-mail letter on page 31 and get to work on your own letter.

It's almost like going to a bookstore not quite sure what book you want to buy.

Bright Idea

Ask your friends, neighbors, and business associates to save any direct-mail pieces they have found interesting and that compelled them to open the envelope. Start a file and save them; review the file at least twice a year.

Sample Direct-Mail Letter

September 12, 2002

Dear Executive Director,

Did you know that in the next 90 days more than $10 million will be donated to nonprofit agencies in Delaware by local foundations? Do you know how to apply for your fair share of these funds?

My name is John Riddle, and I have over ten years' experience as a fund-raising professional. I have worked at nonprofit agencies in Delaware, Maryland, and Pennsylvania as a development director, director of special events, and vice president of public relations.

If you need temporary fund-raising help for a day, a week, or a few months, call on an experienced fund-raising professional to help you meet your fund-raising goal. Why not give me a call today? Together we can develop a plan of action that will work for your agency.

Sincerely,

John Riddle

John Riddle
Fund-Raising Consultant

So what do you do? Well, you spend some time browsing, looking for something that jumps off the shelf and says "Buy me!" Publishers who go the extra mile doing market research into what makes consumers pick up a book know the importance of having just the right color, the right design, and the right copy written inside the jacket. Those are the important features a consumer is looking for when they are shopping for a new book.

When I teach my Introduction to Freelance Writing workshop, I always have the class meet at least once at a large bookstore in town. The students usually laugh and joke about going on a field trip at their age, but when I show them why customers stop and pick out certain books off the shelves—while totally ignoring other titles—they begin to realize just how serious this field trip is.

Tip

Smart Tip

If you need to hire a freelance writer, contact your local newspaper to see if there are any writing clubs or associations that meet in your area. You could also check the various writing Web sites on the Internet; they will be a valuable resource if you need professional writing assistance.

You see, if you are a writer and want to sell a manuscript to a publisher, it makes good sense to select a publisher based on how well they have put together their books for sale in your local bookstore. Think about it: if a book publisher has gone that extra mile and invested the time, energy, and resources necessary to come up with a title that screams "Buy me!" then that is the publisher to whom you want to sell your manuscript.

The same rule holds true for direct-mail pieces. When you receive some that scream "Open me!" then the writer, designer, and graphic artist have done their jobs—and done them well. So now you know that you need to have a dynamite direct-mail piece advertising your consulting business and services. Period. No excuses. You will have one sooner or later, so you might as well make it sooner, and get it done right!

If writing the perfect brochure or direct-mail letter scares the daylights out of you, hire a professional writer. A really good direct-mail piece is worth its weight in gold. So don't cut corners when it comes time to do yours! See page 33 for a sample brochure.

For more on direct mail, read Chapter 20 in Entrepreneur's *Start-Up Basics*.

Brochure Basics

There are five issues your brochure should address. They are:

1. It should clearly convey what your services are.
2. It should tell customers why you are the best.
3. It should give a few reasons why you should be hired.
4. It should include some brief biographical information.
5. It should include some information about who your other clients are.

That's it. Keep it simple, but do it right. Remember, your brochure represents you in the marketplace, so make sure you polish it before you send it into action. Your entire consulting career depends on it.

Sample Brochure

L R S MARKETING

GOES TO WORK AS YOUR:

- ◆ Project Planner
- ◆ Document Designer
- ◆ Writer
- ◆ Artist
- ◆ Publicity Partner
- ◆ Quality Assurance Team

We will be there for you!

L R S MARKETING INC.

L R S MARKETING INC.

MARKETING/
ADVERTISING
CONSULTANTS

"Reach For The Stars"

Tel: 302-994-2147

ABOUT US...

L R S Marketing Inc. was founded in 1996. Its staff has over 23 years of marketing and advertising experience.

Since its founding in 1996, L R S Marketing has been devoted to upgrading the quality of marketing and advertising in this highly competitive market.

When you hire L R S Marketing, you're hiring a ready-made team of specialists that can make a difference in your business. All the components are in place: project manager, copy writers, editor, media and advertising consultants.

We hire experience, and all of us are great fun to work with.

"Gentlemen start"

Let L R S Marketing assist you in all the phases of marketing your company or products.

WHAT WE DO...

We will meet with you to assure your comfort and satisfaction. Together with you, we create

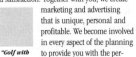

"Golf with the"

marketing and advertising that is unique, personal and profitable. We become involved in every aspect of the planning to provide you with the personal attention you deserve. L R S Marketing provides an invaluable service to companies. As full-time consultants, we concentrate on your needs. We have creativity, organizational skills and a very professional approach. These qualities are necessary to create the perfect plan!

Project Planning And Management

We plan your documents, analyze the audience needs, define its contents, generate outlines, design the document, as well as schedule and budget the project.

Writing

L R S Marketing writes the drafts, revises text, incorporates review comments, writes the final draft and sends it off to the printer.

Editing

We edit the text for consistency, accuracy and usability. L R S will assist with preparing your artwork and integrating it with your text.

"And they're off"

Quality Assurance

We test your documents for accuracy and completeness.

L R S MARKETING INC.

1915 East Zabenko Drive
Wilmington, DE 19808
Phone: 302-994-2147
Fax: 302-994-2147
Email: Roxy1102@aol.com

Cold Calls

If the thought of making cold calls gives you the shivers, then you'd better hire someone to do your marketing for you. Making cold calls can actually be fun; it all depends on your attitude.

The key thing to remember about making cold calls is this: You don't have to make that many if you don't want to. Cold calls are just one more method in the marketing mix. But even if you're not exactly jumping for joy at this aspect of marketing, it will pay to learn as much about successful cold-calling as you possibly can.

To be successful making cold calls to potential clients, you must be prepared to be rejected. It's nothing personal; it's just the nature of the beast. Say you decide on a

---

Warming Up to Cold Calls

You must do whatever it takes to make cold-calling work. There are a few tricks you can use to make it a little easier for you:

○ Prepare a script ahead of time. Spell out word for word what you expect to say when you get someone on the telephone. Remember, though, that your goal is to get a face-to-face interview and, eventually, a new client. So before you end up stumbling over your sales presentation (either in person or over the telephone), write your script and practice it again and again.

○ Be creative in your efforts to reach the decision maker. Most times you will encounter a secretary or administrative assistant who has years of experience turning away cold callers like yourself. But don't give up. Don't let any obstacle stand in your way. (One of Winston Churchill's favorite sayings was "Never give up, never give up, never ever give up!" Don't you think that should be your favorite one, too?) To avoid being screened by the secretary, try calling before she is on the job. Yes, you may have to call before 8 A.M. or after 5 P.M., but at these times, chances are the decision maker you are trying to reach will answer their own telephone.

○ Limit your cold calls to just several days each month. And look forward to those days, making sure you put your best effort into the process. That way, not only will it become easier to make those cold calls, but you will find yourself actually looking forward to making them.

Beware!
Be sensitive to what time of day you are making any cold calls. Remember how you react when you receive this type of call! Never call at dinnertime, and be aware of any difference in time zones.

Monday morning to begin your day by making cold calls to obtain the clients you need to keep your business in a healthy cash flow situation. In order to get at least one prospect to say "yes," you may have to make between 20 and 30 contacts with the people who have the authority to hire you.

Yes, you did read that figure correctly. In order to get at least one yes, you will have to experience an awful lot of nos. Depending on your fee schedule, that figure could be higher or lower. One good marketing option you have when making those cold calls is to be flexible with your rates. In other words, do whatever it takes to grab that client.

When I was working as a fund-raising consultant, I published a series of fund-raising newsletters for the nonprofit industry. Every month, my newsletters had just one page of advertising, offering fund-raising products and services of interest to people and organizations who needed to raise money for their various causes.

My usual way of soliciting advertising clients was via direct mail. And during most months, I had no trouble selling enough ads to fill up that section. But on occasion, I would have to make some "cold calls." In other words, I needed to hustle and sell those ads! Otherwise, I would end up with lots of white space or be forced to use public service ads to fill the void.

So when I made those cold calls, I used every opportunity to make the sale. The most effective one I ever used was when I told the potential customer that there was only one quarter-page ad left and that the usual selling price for an ad of that size was $400. Then I would floor them by saying they could name their own price for that space. Some people would pass on that incredible offer, but most could not resist. The average offer I received for that ad space was between $250 and $350. (I remember one vendor offering me a mere $25 for the ad space; when I asked him if that's all he thought his product was worth, he made a better offer.)

Advertising

The limits you place on advertising your consulting services will be directly tied to your advertising budget. If you are lucky enough to have a very healthy advertising budget, remember that you don't have to spend the money on ads just because you have it to spend. Advertising can be *very* expensive. Jeffery B., the Harrisburg, Pennsylvania, consultant, only advertises in his association's publication. "They publish what is called the *Green Book*, which is a directory of research and marketing consulting businesses around the country. It has helped me generate new business," he says.

Other consultants, such as Merrily S. in Newark, Delaware, depend on word-of-mouth. "The best form of advertising [for my business] has been word-of-mouth and recommendations from other people," she says.

Depending upon the type of services you offer, it may be necessary to advertise in specialized trade journals or magazines. For example, as a fund-raising consultant, I have placed ads in such publications as *The Chronicle of Philanthropy, Non-Profit Times* and *Fund Raising Weekly.*

Before you spend any money, start looking through professional journals and newspapers relative to the fields you specialize in. Take some time and examine ads that have been placed by other consultants, and then carefully determine how effective you think their ads may be. Then design one that suits you best.

Look through several back issues of the publications (if you don't subscribe to those journals or newspapers, visit your nearest university or college library; chances are they will have them in their collection). See how many times other consultants have placed those ads. What type of ads did they use? Were they large display ads? Or did they limit themselves to smaller ads in the publications' classified sections?

Many times a professional publication will produce specialized sections throughout the year for its readers. And, more often than not, one of those sections will be a "Consultant's Directory" or "Directory of Consulting Services." As someone who has advertised in those sections in the past, I can tell you they are worth it. So make sure you don't miss out on any of those directory advertising opportunities.

One way you can find out if a particular publication will be producing a directory of consulting services is to contact its advertising department. It will have a yearly calendar available, and you can take some time and plan *your* advertising strategies.

Dollar Stretcher

Contact publications that are directed at your target audience to see if they have any special advertising sections scheduled for production in the next few months. They almost always do, and they may have special discount advertising rates. This is particularly true when it comes to trade newspapers and journals.

Another expensive yet effective way of advertising is in the Yellow Pages of your local telephone directory. Take a look at your own directory to see what types of consultants have already placed ads there. Better yet, when you are at the library looking through back issues of those professional publications, take some time and browse through some telephone books from other cities (you can usually find a large collection of telephone books in the reference section). Again, take a look at the different ads and listings in the Yellow Pages that feature consultants and consulting services.

When you first opened a page that listed consultants, did your eyes go directly to those display ads? I'm sure they did. That's what a display ad is supposed to do—catch your eye and say "Hey, read me first!" The psychology of this is simple. A larger ad will attract more potential clients than a regular classified listing ever will. And people may assume that since you have spent extra money on that display ad, you may be more established and even more professional than those consultants who did not opt for the large ad. If your budget permits, experiment with different sizes of display ads and see which one draws in the most business. If you can't afford to do this kind of experimentation (and many newbies can't), remember that it's entirely possible to create an effective, small-space ad. For more information on advertising, read Chapter 20 in Entrepreneur's *Start-Up Basics*.

> **Smart Tip** *Tip*
>
> Before placing any ads, check to see if the publication offers discounts on certain days of the week (for newspapers) or time of the year (for monthly publications). Many periodicals offer discounts, but only if you ask for them.

Newsletters

Newsletters can be a very effective tool when it comes to getting clients for your consulting business. Through newsletters, you can present news of interest to

Anatomy of a Newsletter

A typical newsletter published by a consultant will include:

○ *News of importance to their industry*: You can collect information from a variety of sources: magazines, newspapers, professional journals, Web sites, etc. Just make sure you credit the source of each news item you use.

○ *Editorials and opinions*: Here is your chance to sound off on a particular subject relative to your consulting field.

○ *Tips for success*: Tell your readers how to do their jobs better.

potential clients and remind former clients that you are still alive and kicking—and available if they need help again.

When I started out as a fund-raising consultant, it became clear to me that publishing a variety of fund-raising newsletters was the most effective means I could possibly use to sign up new clients. After all, my target audiences were nonprofit organizations that needed to raise money. And when you need to raise money, sometimes your available resources will not allow you the luxury of subscribing to professional newsletters. In the fund-raising field, for example, it was not unusual to find a newsletter selling for between $200 and $400 per year. So I began mailing a free six-month subscription to local nonprofit agencies I thought might benefit the most from my newsletter—and that I thought might be good candidates to use my consulting services. Because I controlled what articles appeared in each issue, I could use that space to tell my success stories as a fund-raising consultant for other nonprofits.

My strategy paid off. Within the first year, I received consulting contracts from four nonprofit organizations—all because they had been on my "free" mailing list! Take a look at a copy of my newsletter on page 39. This should give you a good idea what a consultant's newsletter can look like.

Merrily S, the consultant in Newark, Delaware, does the graphics for newsletters for other consultants. "I have consultants coming to me who are doing mainly marketing and PR," she says, "and they want me to design brochures and newsletters for them."

Whatever your consulting field is you should have more than enough information to produce a newsletter as a means of attracting potential clients. If you don't have the time, or don't feel comfortable self-publishing your own newsletter, hire a local freelance writer and graphic designer to do the job for you. Again, you don't have to make it an expensive, four-color, glossy publication. The simpler you keep it, the better. A good newsletter will sell itself based on the *content* rather than the splashy design.

Start collecting newsletters that are being published in your consulting field. If you think there are none being published, or if you think there are only a few in your field, guess again. A quick visit to the library will reveal several newsletter directories—*Oxbridge Directory of Newsletters* (Oxbridge Communications) and *Hudson's Newsletter Directory* (The Newsletter ClearingHouse)—which list, by subject, newsletters that are published not only in the United States, but in other countries. Take some time and write for sample copies before you design and write the first issue

Sample Newsletter

Book Of The Month

Children as Volunteers: Preparing for Community Service By Susan J. Ellis, Anne Weisbord and Katherine H. Noyes. Published by Energize, Inc., 5450 Wissahickon Ave., Philadelphia, PA 19144-5921 Call toll free: 800-395-9800. $14.75 This book shows you how to tap into a high-energy and fun pool of talent: children. Learn how to incorporate children into an adult volunteer program and find creative ways to use children's fresh perspectives. Included are examples of actual volunteer projects accomplished by children, models of child-adult teams, and tips on family volunteering.

Knight Foundation

The John S. & James L. Knight Foundation is located at One Biscayne Tower, Suite 3800, Two South Biscayne Blvd. Miami, FL 33131. Annual Report & Giving Guidesltines are available.

Fundraising Blueprint

1-800-359-2546

FUNDRAISING BLUEPRINT is published monthly by: Blue Moon Communications, Six Basset Place, Bear, DE 19701. A one-year subscription costs $79. Copyright 1996 by Blue Moon Communications.

Fundraising Ideas

$$$ Liberty Travel. Your ship has just come in! For information on how a cruise can help your organization raise thousands of dollars, contact Liberty Travel at 1940 Commerce Street, Suite 209, Yorktown Heights, New York 10598.

$$$ Preston-Hopkinson. For proven fundraising products that commemorate and support your church, contact Preston-Hopkinson at P.O. Box #1, Lynchburg, VA 24505. Since 1949 they have assisted thousands of churches and schools with their fine Porcelain Fotoware.

$$$ RoyaleHouseInc. Signature bricks and tiles are very effective fundraising tools. Contact Jean Avila at RoyaleHouseInc, P.O. Box 606, Racine, WI 53401. Ask for your free fundraising idea kit that will help set your project apart from the others.

$$$ Great American Duck Races. Has your organization held a Duck Race yet? What are you waiting for? They are fun, easy to produce and always make money. Contact Great American Duck Races at 1525 N. Hayden Road, Suite F1, Scottsdale, AZ 85257. Telephone: 602-957-DUCK.

$$$ Lite-America. Sandra Ambrose, President of Lite-America, offers a catalog filled with fundraising ideas. Give her a call at 800-877-8790, or write to P.O. Box 42533, Cincinnati, OH 45242

Resources...

* Auction Information - Contact Benefit Auctioneers, Inc., 21379 Old Barn Lane, Lake Zurich, IL 60047. Timothy Duggan, company president, is an auctioneer and consultant who specializes in benefit auctions. They conduct Benefit Auction Workshops to teach nonprofit groups how to organize and conduct their own successful benefit auctions.

* Volunteer Information Software - Contact BWB Associates, LTD, 10-A South 7th St. Akron, PA 17501. Bruce W. Bechtold, company president, has developed software so easy "you can't mess up!" Call for a FREE DEMO - 717-859-6642.

* Planned Giving - Contact Deferred Giving Services, 614 South Hale St., Wheaton, IL 60187. Consultant David Schmeling offers a planned giving seminar which offers a practical, common-sense approach to a complex subject. Call 708-682-4301 for a list of seminar sites and dates. (If you can't attend the seminar, you can purchase the resources materials.)

Correspondents Wanted

FUNDRAISING BLUEPRINT is seeking correspondents from Florida, Texas, Maine, and California.

If you would like to report on fundraising activities (and receive a free subscription), send a letter of interest to Blue Moon Communications, Six Basset Place, Bear, DE 19701

FUNDRAISING BLUEPRINT

A BLUE MOON COMMUNICATIONS PUBLICATION
MARCH 1996
Vol. 2 No. 3 | Page 1 of 4

This Smiling Face Wants To Give You Money

See page 4 for details.

Editor's Notebook

— John P. Riddle

Nothing is impossible. Especially your fundraising goals. "The one unchangeable certainty," said John F. Kennedy, "is that nothing is unchangeable or certain." The more improbable something is, however, the more work it takes to achieve. If there is something impossible about your fundraising goal, go after it anyway. Remember, one of the greatest pleasures in life is doing what other people say you cannot do. Abraham Lincoln wrote "things may come to those who wait, but only the things left by those who hustle." Thomas Edison said, "everything comes to him who hustles while he waits."

Raising Operating Funds: Difficult, But Not Impossible

Second installment of a three-part series.

There comes a time in the life of every organization when they must seek the elusive "operating support" portion of their budget. Sure, everyone wants to give money for your new building project, or to purchase a new van, or to even buy the latest high-tech computer equipment...but, just hint to a funding source that what you really need is *operating funds*, and suddenly your requests are rejected. Why? Because most corporations and foundations earmark the majority of their contributions for specific programs. (The key word in that statement is *most*.) Your fund-raising mission should include seeking out those funding sources which do provide operating support—while at the same time rallying support for various programs your organization offers. (Research Grant Guides publishes the "Directory of Operating Grants," an excellent list of funding sources which award operating grants. Their address is P.O. Box 1214, Loxahatchee, FL 33470.)

After you have submitted your grant requests to those national funding sources, it's time to target local corporations and small businesses. Many organizations have come up with creative ways to get prospective donors interested in paying for basic operating expenses. One nonprofit agency in Louisville, Kentucky asked a local tire company to pay their monthly telephone bill, which costs almost $5,000 each year. The tire company said yes, which prompted the agency to ask another company to pay their electric bill—and again, they were successful in their request.

Why, do you ask, would a company do such a thing? Think about it...most businesses want to help, but many are reluctant to have their money "sent into a dark hole" (which is what many corporations equate operating funding requests to be). The nonprofit agency in Kentucky just sends their monthly bill to the business which has agreed to pay for it. What do you have in your operating budget that you can ask a local business to provide? Printing services? Open the telephone book to the yellow pages and start calling

continued on page 2

Inside This Issue

The Only Direct Mail Rule You Need To Know!

Raising money via Direct Mail can be a great way for an agency to raise money. (It can also be a great way to get an ulcer, if you're not sure of what you are doing.) When some people think about direct mail, they envision an image of mailings with quantities in the hundreds of thousands. However, even if your next mailing consists of only a few hundred pieces, there are some steps you can take to help make your campaign a success. Before you get started, remember the one and only rule of Direct Mail: *There are no rules!* That's it. (Were you perhaps expecting some elaborate mathematical equation, or the recipe for some magical pixie dust to sprinkle over your envelope? Sorry, but they don't exist.)

A recent trip to the library resulted in dozens of direct mail tips all "guaranteed to produce successful results." Here are just a few:

"Write short letters..."

"Write long letters..."

"Include a premium..."

"Don't include a premium..."

"Use a fancy envelope..."

"Use a plain envelope..."

continued from page 1

printers—you will find one (or more) who will be willing to donate a project or two. Many of the largest nonprofit agencies in the country receive almost 50% of their operating budget as non-cash gifts or in-kind donations. What have you got to lose? (Just another line item in you budget, that's all!)

Next Month: Planning Ahead for Survival.

With so much conflicting advice on the market today, it's no wonder nonprofit agencies have trouble producing the best direct mail appeal which is right for them. Remember, figuring out what works in direct mail appeals is an inexact science at best. Consultants, experts, professional copywriters and others all have different—and sometimes conflicting—ideas about what's most important to include in a direct mail fund-raising letter.

Try this little experiment: For thirty days collect all of the charitable appeals you receive at home. And ask five friends to do the same. At the end of the thirty days count the number of solicitations (should be close to 100). Ask your friends which ones they thought were appealing (and which ones they would have thrown away without even opening). Do the same yourself. The point to this little experiment? You now have in your possession some successful examples of direct mail to use as basis for your own campaign.

Fundraising News

• Microsoft Corporation is giving over $10 million dollars worth of software to the United Negro College Fund. They will donate Windows 95 and Windows Office software packages to the 41 colleges and universities that are members of the fund...

• An On-Line Silent Auction raised more than $3,500 for an airlift to Bosnia by AmeriCares, the international relief organization. For more information, contact John Johnson, Web Consultant, Online Computer Market, 313 Speen St., Natick, MA 01760...

• According to a Harvard University professor, television is the major reason people are becoming less and less likely to join voluntary associations. In the winter issue of *The American Prospect*, professor Robert D. Putnam reports that people who read newspapers regularly tended to be heavily involved in community activities, while those who watch a lot of television are not...

• Donors under the age of 30 are more demanding of the charities they support than are older people, according to a poll conducted by the Non-Profit Council of the Direct Marketing Association. More than three-quarters of young donors said they wanted to see a charity's internal documents, such as financial reports and strategic plans, before deciding whether or not to get more involved with the organization. For further information, contact the Direct Marketing Association Non-Profit Council, 1120 Avenue of the Americas, New York, NY 10036...

• Cartoonist Garry Trudeau (Doonesbury) is using the Internet to persuade his fans to get involved as donors and volunteers to four of his favorite charities. For more info, contact Richard Shell, President, The Doonesbury Company, P.O. Box 67, Sausalito, CA 94966...

Country Line Dance Event A Huge Success

For the second year in a row, Junior Achievement of Delaware closed a local bridge on a Saturday afternoon to allow several hundred people to participate in a unique fundraising event. People were boot scootin' and stomping more than 136 feet above the Chesapeake & Delaware Canal in the middle of the Reedy Point Bridge. While the view was breathtaking, the wind sometimes forced everyone to hold onto their hats as they performed various country line dances. Officials at Junior Achievement sold T-shirts which served as the "admission" to the event. And not everyone who participated had to dance on the bridge. A few hundred people bought their T-shirts and participated by satellite at several night clubs and convention centers throughout Delaware. The event raised almost $7,000.

Foundation Tips:

* Before submitting your grant request, always write and ask for an annual report and giving guidelines. Many foundations receive thousands of grant requests for programs they don't fund.
* Contact an agency who recently received funding for a program from a foundation you are considering. Many Development Directors are willing to share their success stories with you. This type of networking paid off for an agency in New England which recently received a large grant from Ronald McDonald's Children's Charities.

Recent Grants...

McKnight Foundation - $50,000 for operating support to Walker West Music Academy (St. Paul, MN).

Conrad N. Hilton Foundation - $300,000 for operating support for the Prevention of Sexual & Domestic Violence (Seattle, WA).

Pew Charitable Trusts - $50,000 for adult day-care services at Adult Day Care of Chester County (West Chester, PA).

Robert Wood Johnson Foundation - $15,000 to add a food storage room to its soup kitchen facility at the Trenton Area Soup Kitchen (Trenton, NJ). $90,000 to purchase a new ambulance and communications equipment for the Plainsboro, NJ, Rescue Squad.

Ronald McDonald Children's Charities -$20,000 for a game room for the Boys & Girls Club of Fort Wayne (IN). $10,000 for the youth activities center at the YMCA in Grove City (PA). $25,000 to construct a play therapy room for the Parent Child Center of Tulsa (OK).

New England Foundation for the Arts -$25,000 to expand an arts apprenticeship program for Artists in Humanity in Boston (MA).

Foundations

Robert Wood Johnson Foundation
Route One and College Road East
P.O Box 2316
Princeton, New Jersey 08543
Average grant amount: $85,000.
Areas of interest: Health & Medicine; Hunger; Mental Health; Substance Abuse.

Conrad N. Hilton Foundation
100 West Liberty, Suite 840
Reno, NV 89501
Average grant amount: $150,000
Areas of interest: Domestic Violence; Elderly; Health & Medicine.

Pew Charitable Trusts
One Commerce Square
2005 Market St., Suite 1700
Philadelphia, PA 19103
Average grant amount: $150,000
Areas of interest: Arts; Children; Youth & Families; Elderly; Health; Community Development.

McKnight Foundation
600 TCF Tower
121 South Eighth Street
Minneapolis, MN 55402
Average grant amount: $50,000
Areas of interest: Children, Youth & Families; Arts; Education.

Ronald McDonald Children's Charities
McDonald's Plaza
Oak Brook, IL 60521
Average grant amount: $25,000
Areas of interest: Arts; Children; Music; Recreation; Health; Libraries.

New England Foundation for the Arts
The Fund for the Arts
330 Congress Street, Sixth Floor
Boston, Massachusets 02210
Average grant amount: $20,000
Areas of interest: Art & Culture

of your own newsletter. You'll be surprised at the quality of the newsletters that are being produced today.

Newsletters are an effective means of communication and, in my opinion, represent the best advertising media for a consultant to sell his or her services. Think about it the next time you receive a newsletter in the mail. Did you put it aside to read it later? If so, why did you do that? Probably because you wanted to make sure you weren't missing any important news or information.

But what about that brochure you received in the mail the same day? Did you put it aside to read later? Or did it go directly into the trash can?

Think about this before you spend big bucks on a glitzy brochure that may not even be read. Newsletters rule!

Public Speaking

Public speaking is another excellent way to recruit new clients and to earn a reputation for excellence in your commnity. Unless you live in a town so small it doesn't have a chamber of commerce or a Lion's Club, Rotary Club, or other similar service organization, you can begin offering your services as a speaker for luncheons, dinners, or any other special occasion.

In addition to using the telephone directory, see if anyone has published a directory of service organizations in your community. You can visit the library and ask at the reference desk (by now, I hope you know what an invaluable place the library is and what a valuable resource the librarians can be). Go through and make a list of organizations that hold monthly meetings and therefore may use guest speakers. Contact each group and offer your public speaking services.

As a fund-raising consultant, I am asked to speak to many organizations and talk about the many successful projects for which I have raised money. On several occasions, there were people in the audience who were volunteers

---

Smart Tip

Some service organizations that are always looking for public speakers include:

1. American Legion
2. Lion's Club
3. Rotary Club
4. Kiwanis Club
5. Chamber of commerce
6. Elk's Lodge
7. Masons
8. YMCA/YWCA
9. PTA organizations
10. VFW chapters

or board members from other nonprofit organizations. When the function was over, they approached me about working as a consultant for their agency.

So unless you are deathly afraid of public speaking (and you'd better not be, because as a consultant, you will be presenting oral and written reports for your clients), get busy and start contacting those local service organizations.

The Importance of Associations

If you expect to do business in your community, you need to belong to several associations. When I became a fund-raising consultant, I joined the National Society of Fund Raising Executives as well as the Delaware Association of Nonprofit Agencies. Memberships in both organizations kept me in touch with the majority of the people and nonprofit agencies within my state that could eventually become clients of mine.

> ### Bright Idea
> Check the calendar section of your local newspaper and magazines; it usually lists clubs and organizations that are having meetings and luncheons. A telephone number and a contact name will probably be listed; take advantage of this free resource.

And through my network of contacts and attendance at various luncheons and other events, I obtained plenty of contracts. As a consultant, you can't expect to just sit in your office, send out brochures, and wait for people to beat your door down. You need to get out and be with people—especially the people who have a need for your consulting services.

Melinda P., the independent consultant in Arlington, Virginia, thinks it's very important to network with associations in the field in which you are working. "As a public relations consultant who has done work for many book publishers, I keep in touch with people in the industry," she says.

If you are not sure what associations have a chapter in your city or town, check with the library. It will have a copy of the *Encyclopedia of Associations* (Gale Research Co.). Believe it or not, there is an association for just about every activity and interest in this country today. So as you are browsing through the listings (they are alphabetized by association, as well as grouped by subject matter), copy down names and telephone numbers of the ones you would like to contact.

A quick call to the association's main office number (most will have a toll-free number listed) will reveal whether there is a chapter in your area. If you come across an association that does not have a group meeting where you live, you might consider starting a local chapter. What better way to attract potential clients?

Don't Hesitate to Ask for Referrals

This often-overlooked method of finding new clients is such an easy marketing tool (which is why it's usually not thought of), you'll kick yourself for not thinking of it yourself. When you have finished your consulting assignment and your client is in seventh heaven (and is no doubt singing your praises), that is an excellent time to *ask for a referral.* Simply send a note or a short letter asking for the names of any colleagues, friends, or business associates they feel might be good prospects for your consulting services. Ask their permission to mention their name when you write to the people whose names they pass on to you. Sometimes all it takes is having a mutual friend or respected business associate to get the potential client's attention.

It's also a nice idea to send a letter to clients on their birthdays—or any other noteworthy occasion—to wish them a happy (fill in the blank) and to remind them that you appreciate their business and are available for work. See the sample special occasion letter on page 43 for an example.

The simple thank you letter can be your best friend in the consulting business. There's nothing better than a client who remembers you fondly and feels that you really did the best job you could for them—and a thank you letter helps your clients remember you. For a sample thank you letter, turn to page 44.

Publicity vs. Public Relations

There is a difference between publicity and public relations. Public relations can include press releases, press conferences, special events, or any other methods used to gain public recognition of an event or an organization. Publicity includes advertisements, fliers and news articles that appear either in print media (newspapers, magazines, trade journals, newsletters, etc.) or in broadcast media (television, cable TV, radio, etc.).

With the proper care and feeding of the local news media, you will be able to get the publicity you need to help keep your consulting business in the black. In both print and broadcast media, editors have space they need to fill each day. It may be in the form of column inches (for newspapers) or broken into two- and three-minute time slots (for radio and television).

The sky is the limit when it comes to getting publicity. In fact, you are limited only by your imagination. If you are just starting out in the consulting business, it will be

LRS Marketing Inc.
1000 East Culver Drive
Wilminton, CA 90006
Phone: (949) 857-2000
e-mail: LRSmarketing@aol.com

February 11, 2002

Robin Passwater
Alarm Data Corporation
2500 Eastburn Drive
Irvine, CA 19000

Dear Robin,

Happy Birthday!

Please accept our wishes for an enjoyable day and a prosperous year.

We also want to take this opporunity to thank you for your business. Customers like you make it all worthwhile.

Congratulations again,

Roxanne S. Walker

Roxanne S. Walker
President
LRS Marketing Inc.

Sample Thank-You Letter

LRS Marketing Inc.
1000 East Culver Drive
Wilminton, CA 90006
Phone: (949) 857-2000
e-mail: LRSmarketing@aol.com

February 11, 2002

Randy Reed
ADT Security Service Inc.
18 Boulder Street
Tustin, CA 19720

Dear Randy,

Thank you for participating in the Home Show at the Concord Mall on May 20–23 and also for choosing to do business with LRS Marketing Inc.

Our goal is to serve clients to the best of our ability. If we find more opportunities for your company to exhibit its product, we will be sure to notify you.

Thank you again for selecting us. It is our privilege to work with you.

Sincerely,

Roxanne S. Walker

Roxanne S. Walker
President
LRS Marketing Inc.

Smart Tip

Check with your local media contacts to see if they prefer to have news releases and public service announcements sent via fax, e-mail, or snail mail. By working with the media on their terms, you are enhancing your chances of getting the coverage you desire.

worth your while to obtain the editorial calendars and contact lists for your local media. This way, when you're ready to send something to the press, you have the name of the reporter or editor you need to contact. (Make a quick telephone call to the media to make sure the contact name has not changed. It's not unusual to find that an editor has either moved on to a new assignment or has left that organization altogether.) For more on getting publicity, read Chapter 21 in Entrepreneur's *Start-Up Basics*.

Media Lists

Obtain an up-to-date media contact list to use in all of your publicity campaigns. Contact the chamber of commerce, the Department of Tourism (also known as the Convention and Visitors Bureau in some states) and your local United Way office. Between those three organizations, you should be able to assemble a media list that is all-inclusive.

Keep in mind that there are some important publications that do not appear on the standard media lists. I am referring to corporate and business newsletters. Virtually all large companies publish some type of internal employee newsletter or bulletin. (Check with the human resources departments of the companies you are targeting to see if they have employee newsletters or bulletins.) In addition to featuring news and information of interest to their employees, most of these publications also include community news and a calendar of events.

Let me share a story about how company publications helped me when I worked as a fund-raising consultant.

One of my clients hired me to produce a special event I had come up with. We were going to attempt to make the *Guinness Book of World Records* by having the largest group of people dance the Twist at one time. Since at that time there was no category for doing the Twist, the Guinness people said we had to have at least 5,001 people dancing at one time in order to be in the record book.

The idea was to charge people $5 and have them come to a local race track and enjoy music, food, and fun in the picnic grove. People were encouraged to buy their tickets ahead of time, and before long advance ticket sales were going strong.

While the local newspapers and radio stations were giving us some coverage a few days before the event, I had enormous success from the news releases and stories I had submitted to the various corporate newsletters in town. You see, when the company publications started including news about the event for their employees to read good things began happening.

My client began getting calls from employees who wanted to volunteer for their organization, not only at that event but at future ones as well. And secondly, the corporations were starting to buy large blocks of tickets (at $5 apiece, remember) to distribute to their employees. Many of the employees were able to get tickets not only for themselves but for their friends and family members, too.

When Things Go Wrong

If you have a problem with a client (or even with your own consulting business), it is best not to avoid the media or sidestep their questions. The more you avoid them, the worse it will be.

The fallout from even the smallest hint of scandal can spell disaster with a capital D. You want to avoid being the lead story on page one or on the six o'clock news; people tend to remember bad stories.

With that in mind, it is recommended that you have a disaster plan ready to use in the event something goes wrong. Here are some guidelines for you to use:

1. Always keep the media well informed of all developments of a story.
2. Don't make the media wait for answers to their questions; they may find their own sources for answers, and those other sources may not be accurate.
3. Use only facts. Period. Just facts. Do not give theories, conjecture, or anything but the facts.
4. Update information as often as possible.
5. Maintain a professional attitude.
6. Have just one person be responsible for answering questions from reporters.

For more information on advertising, marketing, and publicity, check out Chapter 20 of Entrepreneur's *Start-Up Basics*.

chapter 5

Prices and Other Money Matters

Have you heard this story before? A newspaper printing plant is in serious trouble. The presses have stopped running, and unless they start again within the next few hours, the newspaper will be delayed and not be available when the sun comes up. The repair people on the job are stumped and cannot figure out why the presses have stopped working.

So they call in a consultant, not worrying about the high fee they will no doubt be charged because of the late hour. It doesn't matter, because the first priority is to get those presses running again.

The consultant comes in, takes a few minutes to examine the printing press, and goes over to one of the gears and taps the gear with a wrench. Within seconds, the presses resume rolling, and the paper makes it to the newsstands just in the nick of time.

When the consultant submits his bill for $1,005, he is asked why he is charging such an odd amount. "Simple," he replies. "It's five dollars to tap the gear and one thousand dollars for knowing which gear to tap!"

So when you set your fees, remember that people are willing to pay you for knowing which gear to tap.

How Much Should You Charge?

Now that you have made the decision to open your consulting business, you need to get serious about how much money you will charge your clients. If you charge too little, you won't succeed in business. If you charge too much, you won't get any clients. So how do you find that middle ground that seems fair to everyone involved? One way to help you decide how much to charge is to find out what the competition's rates are. A simple telephone call, asking for their brochure and rates, should do the trick. Then set your rates so that you are competitive with everyone else in the community.

Bright Idea

Consider sending a survey to a variety of organizations you would like to have as clients. In your survey, ask if they have ever worked with a consultant in the past, and ask them to share as much fee information as they can. And don't forget to ask them if they were pleased with the consultant's performance and if they felt they received their money's worth.

Before setting your fees, make sure you have listed all of your expenses. There is nothing worse than setting your rates, having your client pay you on time, and then finding out you failed to include several expenses that materialized. This brings up an important point to remember in *every* job you take from a client: Include a "miscellaneous" line item in your fee proposal. But don't pad the miscellaneous figure to make additional income.

Most clients will understand that in every project, there will no doubt be additional expenses. Just be sure everyone knows up front an approximate figure for those expenses.

Dollar Stretcher

When you print your brochure or other information about your consulting business, don't include your rates. Keep your prices printed on a special insert. That way, you can change rates without having to reprint the entire brochure.

Before you set your rates, find out what other consultants in your community are charging for their services. Sometimes a simple telephone call to another consultant's office asking what their fees are will give you the answers you need. Or you may have to have a friend call and ask for their brochure, or any additional information they can collect regarding fees and pricing. If you live in a small town and there are no other consultants in your field, then rejoice and be glad, but set your fees at a reasonable level.

When setting your rates, you have several options, including hourly rates, project fees, and working on a retainer basis. Let's examine each one closely.

Hourly Fees

You need to tread carefully when setting hourly fees, because two things could happen: 1) Your hourly rate is so high that no one could ever afford you (therefore no client will ever knock on your door); and 2) your hourly rate is so low that no one will take you seriously.

Keep one important rule in mind when establishing your fee, no matter which structure you decide on: The more money people pay for a product or service, the more they expect to get for their money. In other words, if a client agrees to your hourly rate of $400, then you had better give $400 worth of service to that client every hour you work for them.

Some clients prefer to be billed on an hourly basis, while others hate the idea of paying someone what they perceive to be too much per hour. Those clients usually prefer to pay per project, which we'll discuss shortly.

As a fund-raising consultant, I have had many clients request to be billed on an hourly basis. Since all of those clients were nonprofit organizations, it became clear to me that since a board of directors was ultimately responsible for the financial health of those agencies, they were more comfortable working with a fund-raising consultant who charged by the hour. It makes it easier for some nonprofits to determine their actual fund-raising costs when an hourly billing system is used. Most fund-raising consultants charge between $150 and $300 per hour, depending on the demographics of the community.

Some agencies, however, prefer to be billed by the month.

Project Rates

When working on a project rate basis, a consultant normally gets a fixed amount of money for a predetermined period of time. A few of my fund-raising clients actually preferred to be charged this way, so it wasn't unusual for me to charge $36,000 for a one-year project in which I consulted with them on how they could raise money. Because of the amount of money involved, most agencies preferred to be billed on a monthly basis. This worked out fine until I realized that many agencies were late paying their monthly bills.

Because of this, I decided that all future clients who wished to be billed on a monthly basis would pay the first-month fee and the last-month fee *at the signing of the contract*, which meant that if the agreed-upon amount of the project was $36,000, to be paid on a monthly basis, I received a check in the amount of $6,000 before I began any work ($3,000 for the first month's fee and $3,000 for the last month's fee).

Retainer Basis

Working on a retainer basis gives you a set monthly fee in which you agree to be available for work for an agreed-upon number of hours for your client. While in the ideal world you would have a dozen or so clients who hire you and pay you a hefty sum each month (and never actually call you except for a few hours here and there), don't get your hopes up. Most companies that hire a consultant on a retainer basis have a clause in their contract that prohibits you from working for their competitors.

Working and getting paid in this method certainly has its advantages. You are guaranteed income each month, and when you are starting out in your consulting business, cash flow can be a problem. Some consultants actually offer a percentage reduction in their fees if a client will agree to pay a monthly retainer fee. The average income when a consultant is paid on a retainer basis is $3,500 per month.

Bonus Options

It is not unusual for a consultant to have some type of bonus option in their letter of agreement or contract with their client. A bonus may be a percentage of an amount that the consultant saves a client (if they have been hired to reorganize a department or division, for example), or in the case of my fund-raising clients, a percentage of the amount I raised for them.

About ten years ago, I had a client who approached me and asked if I would work as a fund-raising consultant getting paid only a percentage of any money that I raised for them. While at first I considered the offer, I counteroffered with a small monthly retainer fee and reduced their percentage rate they originally offered. This way, I would receive something each month for the work I would be doing, and I was still guaranteed a bonus.

I ended up charging them $2,000 per month for 12 months and was to receive 10 percent of any foundation or corporate grants I was successful in obtaining for them. So at the end of the first year, I had been paid $24,000 in retainer fees and received a bonus in the amount of $17,000 (which was 10 percent of the $170,000 I raised for them). They

Beware!
Pay quarterly taxes on your earnings, especially if you begin to collect bonuses. You could be in for a real shock if you wait until April 15th to pay tax on any substantial earnings you receive from your clients.

had originally offered me 20 percent (which would have given me only $34,000); so in this case, I ended up earning more with a lower percentage rate and a fixed monthly retainer rate (they paid me $41,000 total, $7,000 more than I would have made if I had opted for the straight 20 percent). It doesn't always work out that way, but again, depending on your cash flow situation, it may work in your favor to have a bonus option. The average bonus is 15 to 20 percent of the funds obtained for the organization.

For more information on quoting prices, read Chapter 25 of Entrepreneur's *Start-Up Basics*.

Should You Accept Credit Cards?

As a consultant, there are some important things to remember about accepting credit cards for the services you provide.

❍ It is a good idea to offer this payment method if you will offer workshops or seminars, or sell subscriptions to a newsletter. Research has proved that people will not hesitate to plunk down their charge card to buy something at a seminar or trade show. But those same people will more often than not hesitate to write a check for that same product or service.

❍ Shop around with local banks to see which can offer you the best rate. In Wilmington, Delaware, for example, where there are more banks than you can count, the rates range from 2 percent to 4 percent, depending on such factors as monthly sales volume and if you have been a commercial customer for some time.

❍ Depending on who your client base is, your regular consulting clients will probably not pay using their credit cards; however, it is better to offer this payment method. Accepting credit cards could put the odds in your favor when a potential client is deciding between your competitor's company and your company. For in-depth information about accepting credit cards, check out Chapter 10 of Entrepreneur's *Start-Up Basics*.

Avoiding Cash Flow Problems

Many consulting businesses have failed simply because they experienced too many cash flow problems. Cash flow problems affect both large and small businesses every

---

Checks in the Mail

Here are five ways to keep the checks coming in while you are between jobs:

1. *Write articles for your local newspaper.* Virtually every newspaper in the United States buys material from local freelance writers. And since you are a professional in your chosen field, you should have no difficulty writing articles for those newspapers. These articles enhance your portfolio and are bound to impress potential clients.

2. *Write articles for trade journals relative to your niche.* If you are a marketing consultant, send articles to marketing journals and magazines. Consider the publications you already subscribe to good candidates for your material. But don't stop at that list (it may be rather short); check out *Writer's Market* (Writers Digest Books) and *Literary Market Place* (R.R. Bowker Inc.) in your local library.

3. *Consider working for a temporary employment agency.* Depending how much time you have available, you may work for a few days or a few weeks to keep money coming in. But if you choose this route, don't forget to keep marketing your services.

4. *Teach a course at your local college.* Check with your local college's employment office to see if there are any openings for an instructor for the noncredit courses they offer. If there are no openings for instructors, consider offering a new course. Another option in teaching a workshop is to offer one free of charge.

5. *Write a book.* Did you know that it is possible to sell a book idea on the basis of just an outline and sample chapter? Writer's Digest Books has several excellent tomes that explain how to get published. By writing and having a book published about the industry in which you have chosen to consult, you will add credibility to your work as a consultant.

day in this country, so don't feel badly if you run into some temporary cash flow problems. There are some ways to avoid the cash flow blues:

Smart Tip

When accepting credit cards, don't stop after MasterCard and Visa. Many of your clients will want to use American Express cards as well. Check with your bank to see what credit card options you can use in your consulting business.

○ Before you sign any contract or letter of agreement, make sure you have double- and triple-checked the budget you have proposed. Go over each line item and expense carefully, because the time to spot trouble is before it begins.

○ Consider asking for the first and last month's fees up front (at the signing of the contract), or at least ask for one-third of the amount you expect to collect. This, of course, will depend on several factors: who your client is, how healthy their cash flow situation is, etc.

○ If your client has failed to keep up their end of the payment schedule, refuse to continue working until payments have been brought up to date. (Make sure you have a clause in your contract or letter of agreement dealing with this problem; otherwise, the client may have you over the legal barrel.)

chapter 6

Being the Best

When you are trying to make a living as a consultant, you want to do everything you can to set yourself apart from the competition. You want to give your clients a reason to say, "We're really glad we chose this consultant." In other words, you want your clients to be happy at every stage of the relationship.

For Roxanne W., the consultant in Wilmington, Delaware, customer service is a top priority. "The more people who know what a good job you do, they will spread your name to other people, and you will end up with more referrals and recommendations," she says.

One way to ensure that the relationship stays happy is to provide the best customer service on the planet (for more detailed information about customer service, read Chapter 22 in Entrepreneur's *Start-Up Basics*).

The best example of outstanding customer service I have ever come across is provided by Stew Leonard, an entrepreneur who owns a store in Norwalk, Connecticut, that's billed as "The World's Largest Dairy." His store, Stew Leonard's, combines elements of Disneyland and Dale Carnegie, and it delivers a straightforward message: *Have fun!*

In his case, fun equals big-time profits—a few years ago Stew Leonard was grossing more than $150 million annually, making his store the most successful supermarket in the country. I have visited Stew Leonard's on several occasions, and unless you actually go there yourself, it's hard to get the real flavor of what Stew Leonard has put together.

Customers go out of their way to shop there, and they all agree that the reason they shop there is because it is fun. Fun is just the tip of the iceberg, however; Leonard's success rests on his scrupulous management and marketing practices, plus a devotion to customer service that borders on the fanatical.

To understand what his customers want, Leonard usually spends an hour or so each day patrolling his grocery store, which stocks around 1,000 items (compared to an average of 15,000 items found in a larger supermarket). His philosophy is simple: he gives the people only what they want—nothing more, nothing less.

People who visit his store never wait in line to check out with their groceries. Leonard makes sure that each of his 29 registers is always open. And he listens to his customers when they tell him something. He treats each person who walks through his doors as if they were royalty because in Leonard's eyes, they are.

One story he likes to share with people is the time a customer came into the store around the holiday season. She was trying to return a carton of eggnog that she claimed was spoiled. Leonard told her that about 300 other customers had bought eggnog from the same batch without a problem. In short, he told her, she was wrong, and she wouldn't be getting a refund.

> ### Smart Tip
> *Tip*
>
> Remember that your customers are the most important aspect of your consulting business; without them, you—and your business—will never survive.

The woman complained that she would never shop there again, and after she left the store Leonard realized what a mistake he had made. In fact, within a few months he erected a monument to his customers and memorialized his own mistake. A three-ton granite boulder stands at the entryway to the store, emblazoned with the store's two cardinal rules. "Rule Number 1: The Customer Is Always Right. Rule Number 2: If the Customer Is Ever Wrong, Go Back and Reread Rule Number 1."

As an entrepreneur, Leonard has won the praise of Fortune 500 executives and been cited by author Tom Peters in his book, *In Praise of Excellence*.

Service with an Ear-to-Ear Smile

1. *Accept full responsibility for all your actions when it comes to consultant-client relationships.* Concentrate on giving your very best, no matter how good, bad, or indifferent your client may be.

2. *Develop an attitude of optimism and positive expectation.* Begin to expect the very best from yourself, and soon others around you will see what a powerful force you present. Remember, optimists are simply people who have learned how to discipline their attitudes to their advantage.

3. *Motivate yourself to have a "never give up" style.* Make your client feel that you are there for them no matter what. In other words, you will go above and beyond the call of duty to fulfill your end of the assignment.

4. *Keep improving your communication skills.* When there is a breakdown in communication, chaos results. Practice your listening skills. Sometimes a client may not be clear about what they want; be certain you understand what is expected of you.

5. *Believe in yourself.* When you have a high level of self-esteem, the sky is the limit.

6. *Be flexible.* Any consultant who can maintain a high degree of flexibility will gain a reputation and have no trouble attracting new clients.

7. *Set goals.* When you have a plan of action, with certain goals in mind, they will be easier to achieve. Remember, if you fail to plan, you plan to fail.

8. *Organize yourself.* This will impress your clients and help you become a much more successful consultant.

9. *Seek more than one solution to a problem.* And always look for creative ways to solve those problems. Walt Disney was a firm believer in the power of brainstorming; you should be too.

10. *Be happy.* When you're happy, those around you will be happy, too.

Now, when you think about offering the best customer service possible, remember Stew Leonard. In fact, your goal should be to top Mr. Leonard's customer service philosophy—if that's even possible.

Develop a Win-Win Style

In order to succeed as a consultant, you need to develop a win-win style of management. This means that both you and your client view everything that is done as something positive, as a means of moving forward, as a way of solving a problem.

Your ultimate success depends on you and your ability to use your inner resources and strengths. You hold the secrets to winning; without unlocking those secrets, you are doomed to failure. Do whatever it takes to solve your clients' problems and challenges. By doing so, both you and your client come out winners.

Melinda P., the Arlington, Virginia, consultant, has some advice for people who are trying to make it in the consulting field. "One thing I would highly recommend, particularly to women who are consulting for organizations, is to get to know what the power structure is in that organization and get to know the support staff as well as your contact person," she says.

> **Bright Idea**
> Your attitude is your most priceless possession and can make the difference between success and failure as a consultant. Take time for an attitude check every day; it should always be in a positive mode.

Five Situations to Avoid

As a consultant, you may feel as if you have to be all things to all people. And sometimes in doing so, you may be setting yourself up to fail. Let's examine five problem areas you need to consider before accepting any consulting position:

1. *You aren't able to identify the real problem.* You need to look beyond your specialty to determine where a client's solution may be. I once had a client whose nonprofit organization had grown out of control. They were having difficulty meeting their monthly bills, and their contributions from foundations and corporations had been steadily declining over the years. Yet they kept growing and offering their health-related services throughout the state. When I first took them on as a client, I thought they simply needed a rock-solid fund-raising plan,

one that would dramatically increase their ability to attract the contributions they needed to stay open. But after carefully interviewing many of their key employees and managers, I realized that their fund-raising plans were OK; they needed a consultant who was skilled in nonprofit reorganization.

Smart Tip

Keep up with the business books published each year. Some of the information will no doubt be helpful to you and your clients.

2. *You promise more than you can deliver.* While every consultant likes to think they can solve everyone's problem on time and under budget, the reality of the business is that you can't. Once you recognize that fact of the consulting life, you won't promise more than you can deliver. It is very easy to sit at a desk and listen to your client talk about their problems. The hard part comes when you need to convince yourself that you can actually solve their problems. If you are not 100 percent sure from the beginning that you can help your client, then don't promise more than you can deliver.

3. *You fail to be specific about the role you will be playing.* Too many times a consultant will sign a contract with a client and really not have a clear understanding of what they are expected to do. Make sure you and your client put in writing what tasks you will be performing and how you will accomplish them. (We'll cover some sample consulting contracts in Chapter 7.)

4. *You fail to treat each client as an individual.* I have seen countless nonprofit organizations spend thousands of dollars on consultant after consultant. And each time the client hopes that the consultant will help them. But the very nature of the consulting industry allows for boilerplate reports and recommendations. Far too often, a consultant will come in, listen to their client's problems and concerns, and already be mentality calculating how many pages their report needs to be. And they are very excited because they know they will be able to use a report that they have presented to other organizations they have worked for in the past. All they need to do, really, is to change the names, dates, and figures. "After all," the consultant thinks, "all of these problems are the same." If you want to succeed in the consulting world, you'd better learn to treat each client, and their problems, individually.

5. *You may not be qualified to get the job done.* Occasionally you may come across a client who offers you a job that you know you would like to have (either for the money or for the prestige of working for that particular client), but you may not be qualified to get the job done. Know when you should take a job, and know when you should turn down a job. If you are offered a job you would never be able to do on

your own, consider bringing in an associate on a temporary basis to help you. (We'll talk more about hiring additional help in Chapter 9.)

As a consultant, it is your job to market yourself and to sell your services to those clients who need your help. Make sure both you and your client are happy with the results.

chapter 7

Contract Pointers

In the old days, people did business on a verbal agreement or a handshake. When someone gave you their word, you knew they would honor their end of the bargain.

Times have changed. No longer can business be conducted without something in writing. After all, who can trust anyone these days, right? You need a written document to protect both parties in any type of business arrangement. Can you imagine buying a house without a contract?

To alleviate any misunderstandings in any type of consulting agreement, a detailed contract or letter of agreement needs to be drawn up and *carefully* reviewed by both parties before anyone signs on the bottom line.

It doesn't matter who you are working for, either. In fact, if you are acting as a consultant for someone you know personally, be extra careful and make sure everything that is expected of you is put into writing. When money is involved, friendships can go sour very quickly.

> **Beware!**
> Listen to your intuition. If something doesn't feel right about what a client wants or expects, make sure every point is clarified in your contract or letter of agreement. Leave nothing to chance.

Decide What You Want

Some people are very talented when it comes to getting what they want out of life. I'm sure you have seen (and admired) those types of people who have no trouble asking for—and receiving—what they want.

The same holds true in your consulting business. Before you take on the responsibilities as a consultant for *any* client, be certain that you know what you want in return. And when you are certain of what you do want, take the necessary steps to make sure your needs are met.

The fine art of negotiating a consulting contract consists of four elements:

1. What the consultant must have in order to get the job done
2. What the consultant would like to have to get the job done
3. What the client must have accomplished
4. What the client would like to have accomplished

Let's examine each point carefully:

What the consultant must have in order to get the job done:

A. Data Requirements

When I consider taking on a fund-raising client, there are expectations that I have before I even get to the first meeting. For example, I know that if the client wants me to develop a fund-raising plan and show them how to raise money from foundations, corporations, small businesses, and/or individual contributors, I need access to certain financial records. I usually ask for budgets, audits, long-range planning reports and lists of all sources of income for the past five years.

B. Monetary Considerations

This is always the easy part (ha!). Once you have set your fees, you should be able to communicate to your client the amount of money you need to have in order to get the job done. The first rule in the consulting business is *be flexible*. (But don't sell yourself short; get paid what you are worth.) So when you decide on a figure, make sure it

> ### Smart Tip
> When you go into your first meeting with your client, have a list prepared of what you need in order to solve their problems. Not only will you impress your client, but you will be able to begin work even more quickly.

includes the dollar amount you must have in order to get the job done in a reasonable amount of time. (When it comes to quoting a figure, leave room for some negotiation; some clients prefer to have you reduce your rates by a few dollars or percentage points. It gives them a feeling of satisfaction.)

> ### Beware!
> Don't set your fees too high; you may pick up a few clients in the beginning, but unless your rates are competitive—and fair—you will fail miserably as a consultant.

What the consultant would like to have to get the job done:

A. Data Requirements

In addition to those items covered in the above section, I would like to have the cooperation of everyone on the board of directors, as well as be able to interview some of their past donors. (But I know I can get results without these additional requirements.)

B. Monetary Requirements

Obviously, every consultant would love to have every client pay the highest possible fees. But you must be reasonable when it comes to money matters; after all, both you and your client are in business. And to stay in business, you cannot let your fee structure rule.

What the client must have accomplished:

When a client hires you to perform consulting services, that client will have certain expectations that they must have fulfilled. It is your responsibility to see to it that all of your client's needs are met. The client must feel as if they are not only getting their money's worth, but they are also getting the job done on time (and under budget).

What the client would like to have accomplished:

In addition to having the job done correctly and under budget, most clients would like to have additional services performed—without cost to them, of course.

So when you are negotiating with your client, keep in mind that they secretly hope that you will be able to provide them with some type of extra service. For example, almost all of my fund-raising clients hint that they would love to have additional information on potential funding sources but are usually reluctant to pay for additional research time. Because of this, I now build in some additional revenue when I quote a fee for the services they contract for and am able to provide the additional data—at what appears to be "no additional charge." Sounds strange, I know, but it is the nature of the consulting business.

The First Meeting

The first client-consultant meeting sets the tone for the entire relationship. Here are some important items to keep in mind as you go to that first meeting:

○ What is your client's personality? Do they have an aggressive, take-charge management style? Or are they more of a "let's get to know each other before we do business" type of person? The sooner you discover their personality, the easier it will be for you to get the job done.

○ What is your client's problem? Do they know what their problem is? Or are you being asked to find out what their problem is and come up with the solution? More often than not, a client will have a good idea of what their problem is and how they want you to solve it. Make sure you agree with your client on what the real problem is before you agree to accept a contract with them.

○ Is your client ready to accept your recommendations? Make sure your client has an open mind and is willing to listen to your recommendations.

○ Can you agree on a timetable? While most clients would like you to solve their problems in a few days, most are reasonable when it comes to giving you the time you need to solve those problems. However, you will sometimes run into a client who has a hard time understanding why you can't solve their problem overnight. Unless you can convince a client at the initial meeting that a reasonable timetable needs to be agreed upon, you might want to reconsider signing any contract with them.

○ Can you outline who will take responsibility for each task? Make certain that everything is spelled out in writing and that the contract clearly states who is responsible for each task.

Here are a few tips to not only help boost your confidence, but to help you leave a favorable impression on your client.

Smart Tip

Let your contract or letter of agreement sit for 24 hours before you sign on the dotted line. Sometimes a good night's sleep will help you see the details you are agreeing to in a whole new light.

○ *Smile and relax:* Take a deep breath and don't sweat the small stuff. Remember, if you look relaxed and happy, your client will be, too.

○ *Make your first impression count:* How many times have you met someone and, for whatever reason, decided you would rather have nothing to do with them? Well, the same holds true in client-consultant relationships: First impressions count. So make yours an excellent one.

○ *Go to the meeting prepared:* Your client will probably ask you some questions to test your knowledge of the subject you claim to be an expert in. So make sure you are up to date on the latest information in your field.

○ *Go to the meeting ready to listen:* Remember earlier on we talked about the importance of listening? Well, the true test of your listening skills will take place at this initial meeting. Here is where your client will talk about what they really want and when they expect it to be accomplished.

○ *Take plenty of notes:* Information will be flying right and left across the room. Take accurate notes, because you will no doubt be presenting a contract or letter of agreement to your client based on the notes you take during the initial meeting.

Interviewing Work Sheet

What better way to learn what your client wants and expects (and how much they are willing to pay for your expertise) than to ask enough questions? Here are 20 questions you should ask a potential client before signing any contract or letter of agreement:

1. Can you define the problem you are experiencing?

_____

_____

2. How long has the problem been affecting your business?

_____

_____

Interviewing Work Sheet, continued

3. Have you taken any steps on your own to solve the problem?

_____

_____

4. Why do you think the problem is occurring?

_____

_____

5. What are your overall objectives on this project?

_____

_____

6. How do you think your problem can be solved?

_____

_____

7. Is your organization committed to solving the problem?

_____

_____

8. Is your organization ready to implement suggested changes?

_____

_____

9. Who will be my designated liaison on this project?

_____

_____

10. When is the latest you would like to have this project completed?

_____

_____

_____

Interviewing Work Sheet, continued

11. When is the earliest you would like to have this project completed?

_____

_____

_____

12. What will your role be during the project?

_____

_____

_____

13. Will you supply me with all the data I request?

_____

_____

14. Have you developed a budget to pay for the changes I recommend?

_____

15. How much have you budgeted to pay for a consultant?

_____

16. Are there any confidential or restricted documents I will be working with?

_____

_____

_____

17. How often can we meet?

_____

_____

_____

18. Can meetings be called as necessary?

_____

19. How often would you like a progress report?

_____

_____

20. When would you like me to begin?

_____

By the time you have asked your client these 20 questions (and recorded their answers), you will have all the information you need to draft your contract or simple letter of agreement.

Contracts and Letters of Agreement

What is a contract? In simple terms, a contract is an agreement between two parties for one party to do something in return for something of value. Contracts can be very simple one-page documents, or they can be 100 pages long or more, depending on their subject matter and how many complicated issues they cover in depth. Some smaller nonprofit organizations prefer signing a letter of agreement over a contract because it seems less formal than a contract; keep in mind, though, that a letter of agreement is still a binding agreement, enforceable by law.

Now that you understand contracts, you think everything will be fine; you type up a contract, present it to your client, they sign it, and even give you a check for partial payment.

Be advised, however, that the law says that either party can terminate a contract if any of the following has taken place:

❍ *Duress:* Either party must not use force or pressure—and that includes both the mental and physical kind—to get the contract signed.

What's In a Contract?

Every contract has three key elements. Not one, not two, but all three elements must be present for the contract to be valid.

1. Each contract must contain an *offer*. An offer is simply something that is proposed by a person or business. (For example, some of my fund-raising clients prefer a contract over a letter of agreement, so the offer read something like this: *"...will act on behalf of the XYZ nonprofit organization as a fund-raising consultant in order to raise the necessary funds required..."*)

2. Each contract must contain acceptance. Acceptance is when one party accepts the terms *offered* in the contract. (It is usually a good idea to put a time limit on any contract—or even simple letter of agreement—you offer a client. For example, when I present a contract to a new fund-raising client, I tell them that the offer will expire in a set number of days unless it is signed and accepted.)

3. Each contract must contain *consideration*. This means payday. For example, the contract will read something like *"...in exchange for a monthly payment of $5,000..."*

○ *Fraud:* If either party intentionally misrepresents themself or something they promise to deliver (or pay for), then *fraud* is present. And when fraud is present, the contract can be null and void.

○ *Legal:* The contract you are about to sign *must* be for a transaction that is *legal.* For example, if I put in my contract to my fund-raising clients that I would use any means necessary to raise the funds they need—including stealing, if the need presented itself—then the contract would be no good.

○ *Capacity:* Each party who enters into the contract must be of legal age, sound mind, and not under the influence of alcohol or drugs. (I cannot imagine any consultant signing a contract under these conditions, can you? But, you have been warned.)

○ *Full disclosure:* If either party fails—on purpose—to disclose a key piece of information, the contract will be unenforceable.

Sample Contract for Services

This document outlines the agreement made on __(date)_____ for services rendered by John Doe, hereinafter referred to as the CONSULTANT, and _____(name of the person in the organization)_____, as represented by____(name of the person signing the contract)_____, hereinafter referred to as the ORGANIZATION.

1. Statement of Work: During the terms of this Agreement, the CONSULTANT will perform services as requested by the ORGANIZATION from _____(date services will begin)_____ and ending upon _____(date services will terminate)_____ .

2. Travel Arrangements: (If your client is in your hometown and no travel is required, then simply omit this section.) The CONSULTANT will be arriving on ___(date you will be arriving)_____ and departing on ____(date you will be leaving)_____and requests that the ORGANIZATION make hotel reservations that are billed directly to the ORGANIZATION for the night(s) of ___(nights you will be staying in the hotel)_____ . Please secure late arrival and the ability to charge meals and telephone calls to the hotel room.

3. Payment: The ORGANIZATION shall pay the CONSULTANT according to the following schedule:
   a. The fee of ____(agreed-upon fee)_____made payable to the CONSULTANT as agreed upon in writing by both parties with additional expenses being paid by the ORGANIZATION. (If you fail to mention who is paying for additional expenses not covered by your fee, you run the risk of having to cover

Sample Contract for Services, continued

those expenses yourself.) The fee schedule is as follows: _____(Outline in detail when you wish to receive payment; otherwise, some clients will send you a check whenever they feel like it. What I normally do for my fund-raising clients is to specify that a payment is due on the first working day of the month and that if a payment has not been received within 10 days, I reserve the right to temporarily halt any work until such payment has been made.)

4. Relationship of Consultant. The CONSULTANT will serve as an independent contractor and will be responsible for all income taxes.

5. Interpretation of Agreement: This agreement may not be changed except in writing, signed by the CONSULTANT and an authorized official of the ORGANIZATION. This contract contains the specific terms of the agreement as governed by the laws of the state in which the ORGANIZATION resides.

6. Specific Needs. The CONSULTANT will provide _____(specify the type of consulting services you will provide)_____ services to the ORGANIZATION.

7. Consultant Needs: The CONSULTANT will require the following documentation to complete the terms of the contract: _____(Simply state what information you require from your client to get the job done; for example, I talked earlier about how I need certain financial and fund-raising records to develop a fund-raising plan—this is where I would list those needs.)_____

8. Cancellation Clause: Either the CONSULTANT or the ORGANIZATION may terminate this contract by serving notice in writing. A ten-day notice is required to cancel a contract before the term of the contract has expired. (The number of days can be any number you and your client agree on; ten days to two weeks is the norm in the industry.)

In Witness Whereof the Parties hereto have executed this Agreement as of __(date you sign the contract)_____. Please return two signed copies of this Agreement to the CONSULTANT no later than five business days after receipt.

ORGANIZATION:

Name _____
                                    (signature)

Title _____   Date _____

CONSULTANT:

John Doe _____
                                    (signature)

Sample Letter of Agreement

Letter of Agreement

1. In exchange for a one-time fee of $5,000 and 10 percent of any grants or contributions received from foundation or corporate sources, John Doe will submit grant requests, along with supporting documentation (which will be supplied by the organization) to 50 different funding sources.

2. John Doe will deliver the letters and grant proposals, ready for the organization's signature, no later than March 31st (or some other agreed-upon date). Postage costs will be the responsibility of the client.

3. The organization will pay John Doe 10 percent of any foundation or corporate grant money that is received within ten working days of receiving any checks. This 10 percent clause will remain in effect for one year and will expire on March 31, 2000.

4. John Doe warrants that he is qualified to research funding sources and write grant request letters and proposals. The client understands that the appropriate foundations and corporations will make the funding decisions and that no promise is made as to how much money will be raised.

5. There is no limit on the amount of funding that the client can ask for. However, based on research, John Doe will advise the client as to the appropriate amount to solicit as a grant or corporate contribution.

6. The client will pay John Doe a check in the amount of $5,000 on March 1, 1999. Within ten days of receiving the check, John Doe will deliver the first batch of fund-raising letters and grant proposals ready for the client's signature. The remaining letters will be delivered no later than March 31, 1999.

This letter of agreement is in effect upon the signature of both parties.

The above terms are agreed to and accepted by:

_____

client signature and title   *date*

_____

consultant signature and title   *date*

chapter 8

Writing a Winning Report

To be an effective consultant, you must learn how to get your message across to your clients. When you find the ideal solution to their problem, you want to be able to present it in a written format that is easy to understand.

You need to be a good communicator in order to be a good consultant; and you need to be able to express yourself in a solid, winning report that spells out in detail your findings and recommendations.

As a consultant, you will need to provide periodic updates to your client in writing. This helps keep the lines of communication open and helps avoid any potential problems. Your update can be as simple and direct as this sample report I once used for a fund-raising client.

Smart Tip

If you have any close friends or business associates who have used consultants in the past, ask them to let you see a copy of the written report that was submitted by the consultant they hired. That will give you a firsthand look at some reports that have been used.

Sample Consulting Report

Fort Delaware Society
Fund-Raising Report
August 15, 1997

After carefully studying the Fort Delaware Society's position as a nonprofit agency in the State of Delaware, the following fund-raising plan has been drafted for your review. It is recommended that the board of directors carefully review each item, and decide if, and when, they would like to proceed.

While no fund-raising plan is guaranteed or foolproof, this one is designed to raise $26 million for the Fort Delaware Society over the next three years.

1. *Private Foundation Support: $24 million*

    Delaware's largest foundations include: Longwood, Welfare, Laffey-McHugh, Marmot, Crystal Trust, Delaware Community Foundation, Sharp Foundation, Beneficial Foundation, and Life-Enrichment Foundation. The top foundations—Longwood, Welfare, Marmot, Laffey-McHugh, and Crystal Trust—should be solicited for a total of $3 million a year over three years. The remaining Delaware foundations should be solicited for a total of $1 million a year over three years.

    (Total: $12 million)

    Other foundations that have a history of funding projects like the renovation and restoration of Fort Delaware include: Pew Charitable Trusts, AT&T Foundation, Fidelity Foundation, Chrysler Foundation, Merrill Lynch Foundation, Abell Foundation, Newman's Own Foundation, F.M. Kirby

Sample Consulting Report, continued

Foundation, Allegheny Foundation, Cafritz Foundation, Andrew Mellon Foundation, Stern Foundation, Wray Trust, Heinz Endowments, J. Paul Getty Trust, and the Turner Foundation. There are dozens of others, but these should be contacted first. Collectively, you should request $4 million a year over three years. (Total: $12 million)

Note: Fort Delaware also qualifies to request money from additional foundations that participate in the National Standard Grant Application. These foundations have joined together to make the application process simple. Once a master application has been received, an agency can make copies and send them in to the appropriate foundations on the list. After carefully reviewing the list, it looks as if Fort Delaware has an additional opportunity to solicit 70 foundations. Amounts range from $25,000 to $2 million.

Recommendation: Beginning in November, start soliciting funds from the Delaware foundations, the national foundations, and the foundations on the National Standard Grant Application list.

2. *Corporate and Business Support: $1.75 million*

    Partnerships between nonprofit agencies and businesses are slowly beginning to mature and take important directions. While it is the normal procedure to solicit a corporation or small business for a contribution, it is suggested that Fort Delaware set itself apart from the other nonprofit organizations who are constantly sending letters asking for "just a handout." Instead, Fort Delaware should devise a program known as the "Adopt-the-Fort" plan. This plan consists of asking corporations and small businesses to "adopt" a section of the Fort (Sally Port, Blacksmith Shop, etc.). The "adoption" process not only involves them contributing money, but providing volunteers and in-kind donations as necessary. (For example, suppose First USA Bank adopts the Fort for one year. It may donate $20,000 and supply volunteers from their employee committees. They may also contribute other items on your wish list, as needed. They would also be in a position to host a picnic for their employees at the Fort, thereby increasing the number of visitors and increasing Fort Delaware's mailing list.)

    Different businesses could adopt the Fort at the same time. These types of "adoption" plans have been successfully done with schools and businesses throughout the country. Very few other nonprofit agencies have yet to try this approach; Fort Delaware has an opportunity to be on the cutting edge and lead the way in Delaware with a new approach to corporate and business giving.

    Recommendation: Beginning in January, start soliciting the top 500 corporations and small businesses in New Castle County to participate in the "Adopt-the-Fort" plan.

Sample Consulting Report, continued

(I have the list of the 500 top corporations and businesses.)

Important Note: Random surveys were taken during the past 90 days, and unfortunately, out of 1,000 people surveyed, only 167 had ever heard about Fort Delaware or Pea Patch Island. By going forward with the "Adopt-the-Fort" plan, hundreds of thousands of Delawareans would be exposed to the Fort.

3. *Special Events: $150,000*

A "Walk For The Fort" event should be held in the fall of 1998 (mid to late September). Because of the uniqueness of Pea Patch Island and the Fort, this type of walkathon should attract approximately 1,000 walkers. Each walker would be required to raise a minimum of $100 to qualify for an incentive prize (T-shirt, sport bottle, etc., with the Fort Delaware logo and logo of the corporate sponsor that provides the prize). Additional money can be raised through other sponsorship opportunities (signage, refreshments, entertainment, etc.). This day-long event will again raise greater awareness of the Fort to the general public.

Recommendation: For this event to be a success, a walk committee should be formed no later than January 15th. I can provide an entire "how-to" kit, which lists the steps necessary to hold a successful walkathon.

4. *Miscellaneous: $100,000*

Other ways to generate fund-raising dollars include:

○ *Direct mail*: Using both the current Fort Delaware mailing list, and a new prospect list, solicit funds with a two-page letter and an information sheet about the Fort. (Start this campaign in March 1998; I will supply a new prospect list.)

○ *Sponsorships/advertising*: Offer corporations an opportunity to advertise at the Fort when it is open. Many businesses would be willing to pay top dollar to have their signs, banners, etc., at such a unique location. This is fairly easy to implement: simply contact advertising agencies in the tri-state area, and they will take care of selling the idea to their clients.

○ *Sell pieces of property*: (On paper only, of course.) Just in time for the holidays, people will be able to give a unique gift to their loved ones. No more fruitcakes, ties, slippers, etc. Instead, for only $25, they can "buy" a certificate (printed on old-time parchment paper, to look like it has been around awhile) that says they own a "piece of property." This has worked well with people who "buy" stars out of the sky and only receive a certificate with their name on it. They could be sold in a variety of ways: at the mall; from

Sample Consulting Report, continued

your Web site; on QVC (home shopping network, always looking for something "different"); or at selected gift and novelty shops in the area. You could even market them through schools and other nonprofit agencies and offer them the opportunity to make $5 on each certificate they sell. You would receive less money but would make up the difference in volume.

Fund-Raising Report

August 1, 1997

By mid-September, the research for your Capital Improvement Campaign should be completed. The research will be divided into several categories: Foundations (Delaware, Regional, and National), Corporations, and Small Businesses. In addition, we will explore the possibility of holding a major special event in mid-1998.

Delaware Foundations—The following foundations in Delaware accept requests for contributions from qualified 501-C3 organizations.

Smart Tip

Write several drafts of your final report for your client. Determine which version will be the easiest to understand. Remember to keep your report simple, using plenty of bulleted facts.

	Average Grant Amount
○ Beneficial Foundation Inc.	$25,000
○ Bernard A. & Rebecca S. Bernard Foundation	$20,000
○ Chichester duPont Foundation Inc.	$35,000
○ Crestlea Foundation	$25,000
○ Crystal Trust	$40,000
○ Delaware Community Foundation	$10,000
○ Ederic Foundation	$50,000
○ Fair Play Foundation	$30,000
○ Good Samaritan Inc.	$15,000
○ Kent-Lucas Foundation	$15,000
○ Milton & Hattie Kutz Foundation	$10,000
○ Laffey-McHugh Foundation	$50,000

	Average Grant Amount
O Longwood Foundation	$250,000
O Life Enrichment Foundation	$15,000
O Lovett Foundation	$15,000
O Marmot Foundation	$50,000
O Sharp Foundation	$35,000
O Welfare Foundation	$75,000

It is strongly suggested that the Possum Point Players submit a request to each of the above foundations for a capital grant. Over the course of the next several weeks, I will prepare additional detailed information concerning the address, deadlines, and what information is required for each application.

Recommendations for the next 30 to 45 days:

O Continue researching other sources of foundation funds. (John Doe)

O Start compiling your mailing list and make sure it includes: vendors, present and past contributors, and patrons. Also, have each board member start making a list of people they know (business contacts, relatives, friends, church, acquaintances, etc.). This list will be added to a database of people who can be solicited for a donation. (Board)

Smart Tip

Tip

In your report, specify who is going to be responsible for each task; unless you specify who is doing what in writing, both you and your client may assume that the other person will be doing the work that is required.

O Develop several special event ideas. (John Doe)

O Develop a list of noncapital funding resources. (John Doe)

chapter 9

Know When You Need Help

When you first open the doors to your consulting practice, you may be able to handle all the operations by yourself. But as your consulting business begins to grow, you may need help handling administrative details or completing the actual consulting assignments.

You need to make some important decisions. For example, do you have the time it will take to make labels and insert your brochure into 1,000 envelopes? Can you afford to spend time doing administrative tasks when you could be using that time effectively marketing your services—and signing up new clients?

There are many options when it comes time to decide if you need help with your paperwork. For example, a quick look through the Yellow Pages will reveal a

Dollar Stretcher

Check with your local community college to see if there are any student interns who will be able to spend time in your office for a few hours each week. That way you get free help, and the student gets some hands-on professional experience.

number of small secretarial support firms. The rates will depend on a variety of factors, including how large or small an organization it is and what types of services it provides.

While it will pay you to shop around for these types of services, don't select a secretarial service just because it happens to have the lowest prices in town. Instead, ask for references, preferably from other consultants who have used their services, or from small-business owners. A good, reliable support service is worth the price in the long run.

There will come a time, however, when you may find it more cost-effective to hire someone to work in the office with you. Hiring a good administrative support person can sometimes mean the difference between success and failure—between obtaining more clients or constantly losing clients. There are some benefits to having someone in the office with you. Among them are:

❍ You save time and money. By having someone concentrate on the more routine tasks (opening the mail, filing, answering phones, etc.) you can focus all your efforts on recruiting new clients. Think about this: Would you want to lose a $500-a-day client because you were too cheap to hire someone to stuff your brochures into envelopes?

❍ You don't worry about being out of the office. If you are a one-person operation, it's hard to be out on the road marketing your services if you're worried about clients calling—and only getting your answering machine.

❍ You have someone to offer another perspective. Sometimes it can be pretty lonely trying to do everything yourself. Having someone around the office during the day who can offer another perspective can be worthwhile.

When you make the decision to hire employees, don't look for potential candidates from among your friends or relatives. If you hire them and they don't

What Time Is Temp Time?

There are several advantages to hiring temporary employees to help out when you're in a crunch. Among them are:

○ You can have a temporary worker for as long as you want them. They are always available to work by the day, week, or month; however often you need them, they will be there.

○ You can avoid the headaches involved in the hiring process. Just pick up the telephone, call a local temporary employment agency, and they will take care of everything for you.

○ The temporary agency pays all of the employee-related expenses: taxes, social security, workers' comp, etc.

○ You only have to pay for the hours they work. There are no headaches or hassles about downtime or paying for vacations.

work out for whatever reason, you not only lose an employee, but a friend or relative, too.

Of course, another option is to use a temporary employee. Sometimes this is the best solution, especially if your consulting business is seasonal. By hiring a temp, you don't have to worry about laying someone off if business is slow.

When your consulting business has grown so large that you need to hire someone on a permanent basis, you obviously want to look for the perfect employee. It doesn't matter if you are hiring a secretary, an administrative person, a bookkeeper, or even an associate who will help you with the actual consulting work. Your goal should be to find the perfect employee. After all, what boss doesn't want an employee who shows up for work early, stays late, and doesn't worry about overtime or comp time?

There is no such thing as a perfect employee. And that's OK, because a perfect person would probably drive you nuts, anyway. So when you are searching for an employee, be sure you have developed an accurate job description that covers all the duties you want the employee to handle.

Many consultants start out as a one-person shop and add employees as their business grows. All the entrepreneurs interviewed for this book started out as, and remain, one-person operations.

How to Write a Job Description

○ Select a job title. Titles may not seem important to you, but to some employees, a title is worth more than the money they are getting paid. For example, you might consider changing "Administrative Assistant" to "Administrative Associate." It doesn't matter that the pay and the duties are the same; the title gives the employee a feeling of prestige and ownership.

○ Outline the *specific* responsibilities the employee will handle. If you don't include everything up front, then you may run into trouble down the road.

- Define the educational experience required.

- Define the additional work-related experience required.

- Establish who the employee will report to.

- If there are any special physical requirements, list them. For example, if your office will be receiving boxes of books that weigh more than 40 pounds each, say so.

> **Smart Tip** *Tip*
>
> Check with your local library and bookstore for publications that show you how to write the perfect job description. A few minutes of effort now will help you avoid problems down the road. Also, check out Chapter 12 of Entrepreneur's *Start-Up Basics*.

Screening Applicants

Because your time as a consultant is valuable, you need to weed out those people who are not qualified. Sure, once you place an ad or let friends and business associates know you have an opening, the resumes will start making their way into your life.

And while an impressive resume may lead you to believe that a candidate is definitely the one you want to hire, guess again. It is easy for a job applicant to make themselves look better than they really are through a well-crafted resume. I am not saying that most people lie on their resumes (although there has been an increase in resume-related fraud over the past decade), but as the employer you need to take with a grain of salt any claims that are made on paper.

If you find someone who is very impressive on paper, just give them a telephone call and talk with them for a few minutes. Screening job applicants by phone will save you wasted hours in the long run.

But before you make that telephone call, jot down a few notes and questions you should be prepared to ask.

- Ask them why they want the job.
- Ask them why they feel qualified to take the job.
- Ask them what their best quality is.
- Ask them what their weakness is.

If after asking those four questions you feel that the person may be a good candidate for your consulting business, make an appointment for an in-person interview.

Howdy, Partner?

Having a business partner is similar to having a spouse. You need to make sure you and your partner agree on everything, never have any fights about money, and have the same dreams and goals. Since no marriage can ever have all the qualities we just described, how can a consultant expect to find a business partner?

It is a difficult decision. If your consulting business has grown to the point where you need additional help, reconsider bringing in a partner unless you absolutely put everything in writing that each partner is responsible for. More partnerships have ended up in court because each one accused the other of doing something wrong, of violating some partnership agreement or contract.

In the beginning, during the so-called "honeymoon period," you and your partner will have no problem getting along. In fact, you will probably begin to think "Heck, why didn't I bring in a partner a long time ago?" Although there are exceptions to the partnership rule (and yes, some businesspeople can be partners without problems), you need to realize that at any given time, your partner could decide to pull out, set up shop for themselves, and literally put you out of business.

It's better to hire an associate consultant—one who is directly under you. Make sure you have a noncompete clause in your contract with your new associate (in other words, if your associate leaves your organization, he or she will be prohibited from starting a consulting business for a specific time period; the standard in the industry is 18 months). The average pay for an associate consultant is $30,000 to $50,000 per year. Good places to look for an associate consultant include professional associations, industry newsletters, and local colleges and universities. Look for enthusiasm, critical thinking skills, and time management skills, and make sure the candidate is a fast learner.

For more information on job descriptions and screening, interviewing, and hiring candidates, read Chapter 12 of Entrepreneur's *Start-Up Basics*.

Beware!

If you decide to take on a partner, make sure that any checks you write require both of your signatures. This will prevent any surprises when it comes to the financial end of your business.

chapter 10

Frequently Asked Questions

The following questions and answers were compiled from two recent conferences: one for the National Society of Fund Raising Executives and one sponsored by the Delaware Association of Nonprofit Agencies.

Q: *I want to open a consulting business, but my city seems to be overrun with consultants. A few years ago, a major corporation trimmed its workforce, and now many of those early retirees are operating as independent consultants. Do you think I stand a chance of succeeding, or should I consider relocating to another city?*

A: Competition among consultants can be fierce, but it also keeps everyone on their toes. When there are a dozen computer consultants in the Yellow Pages, you'd better believe that each and every one of them knows they need to be better than their competitors. And while you may be perceived as the "new kid on the block," that can actually work in your favor. Organizations know that a person who is just starting out in the consulting business will probably charge fees that are much lower than someone who has been around for ten years or longer.

Q: *I am still puzzled about how to set my fees. I feel guilty if I set them too high, but I also feel I may not be able to stay in business if I set them too low. How do I reach a middle ground when it comes to setting my fee structure?*

A: To survive as a consultant in any industry, you need to have fees that will enable you to stay in business; at the same time, both you and your client need to feel that your fees are fair and equitable. Always remember that as long as you provide a service to a client who is willing to pay for your services, and your fees are reasonable (and comparable to others in the industry), you have reached the so-called "middle ground" when it comes to fee structures. So relax and enjoy cashing those checks.

Q: *How important are problem-solving skills to a consultant?*

A: As important as air is to people. Without air, people would perish. Without excellent problem-solving skills, your consulting business doesn't stand a chance of succeeding. You need to feel comfortable and confident that the data you collect will enable you to brainstorm a variety of ways your client can solve their problem. And don't forget to look for more than one solution to a problem; sometimes it may be the second or third idea that turns out to be the best solution to a problem.

Q: *I don't have a lot of capital to start my own business. Should I wait until I have saved enough to open my doors?*

A: Probably not. But the answer will really depend on what type of consulting business you want to open. If you are a fund-raising consultant, for example, the only overhead you will have will be your initial brochure or flier and the postage you use to get the information into the hands of your potential clients. But if you are a computer consultant and need to invest in a wide variety of equipment, then you may run into a problem. However, even if you need money for equipment, explore as many options as possible. For example, it may be worthwhile to lease your equipment in the beginning rather than buying it outright.

Q: *I have always worked as an employee for a large company. I'm not sure I would survive as an independent consultant, but I really want to try. What should I do?*

A: Sometimes making the transition from an employee in a corporate culture to a one-person shop can be a frightening experience. It sounds as if you might do better trying to get a job (even if only on a temporary basis) with a smaller consulting firm. There you will not only gain knowledge and insight into the day-to-day workings of a consulting business, but you will be able to decide if an independent lifestyle is for you.

Q: *I plan to open my consulting business sometime within the next three to four months. Should I wait until I am officially open to begin networking?*

A: Absolutely not. As soon as you are finished reading this guide, start that networking process. Let everyone know the name of your business, the kinds of services you will provide, and when you plan to open your doors. Start researching and collecting names of potential clients. The time you spend now will pay off later.

Q: *How important are writing skills to a consultant?*

A: A good consultant needs problem-solving skills and good writing skills. After all, when you solve your clients' problems, you need to convey to them the results; and although you may make an oral presentation, your client will expect some type of written report from you. So if your writing skills are weak, consider taking a class at your local community college. It will be worth your while and will ultimately help your business grow.

Q: *I am just starting out as a consultant. How can I create a professional image for myself and my business?*

A: Everything from your business cards to your handshake must portray a professional image. Don't make the mistake of trying to be someone you are not; a client will spot a phony a mile away. Be yourself, be open, be honest, and be prepared to go above and beyond the call of duty when providing services to your clients. That should help you establish a professional image.

Q: *How can I find out if there is a code of ethics I should adhere to for the industry I will be consulting in?*

A: Just about every association listed in the *Encyclopedia of Associations* (Gale Research Co.) will have a toll-free telephone number. Call that number and ask for a copy of their code of ethics. Take some time to develop your own code of ethics and live by that code. A good rule of thumb is, if you have your doubts about a decision (with regards to ethics), it probably is not a good idea.

Q: *Do I need to be an expert at time management to have a career as a consultant?*

A: The level of your time management success is directly related to the number of checks you will cash in any given year. In other words, you need to get organized and manage your time well if you want to be a successful consultant.

Appendix

Associations

Airport Consultants Council, 908 King St., #100, Alexandria, VA 22314, (703) 683-5900, <www.acconline.com>.

American Consultants League, 1290 Palm Ave., Sarasota, FL 34236, (941) 952-9290, fax: (941) 952-6024.

Association of Professional Consultants, P.O. Box 51193, Irvine, CA 92619-1193, (800) 745-5050.

Association of Professional Communications Consultants, 3924 S. Troost, Tulsa, OK 74105-4793, (918) 743-4793, <www.komei.com/apc>.

Consultants' Network, 57 W. 89th St., New York, NY 10024, (212) 799-5239, <www.consultants-mall.com>.

National Association of Business Consultants, 6300-138 Creedmoor Rd., #403, Raleigh, NC 27612, (813) 862-0521, <www.nabc-inc>.

National Association of Computer Consultant Businesses, P.O. Box 4266, Greensboro, NC 27404, (800) 313-1920, fax: (336) 273-2878.

National Association of Management Consultants, 5441 Riverdale Rd., #181, Atlanta, GA 30349, (770) 492-2929.

Professional & Technical Consultants Association, 849-B Independence Ave., Mountain View, CA 94043, (800) 286-8703, <www.patca.org>.

Public Relations Society of America, 33 Irving Pl., New York, NY 10003.

Consulting Books

101 Ways to Succeed as an Independent Consultant, Timothy R.V. Foster, Kogan Page Ltd.

138 Quick Ideas to Get More Clients, Howard L. Shenson, John Wiley & Sons.

The Business Plan Guide for Independent Consultants, Herman Holtz, John Wiley & Sons.

The Consultant's Guide to Getting Business on the Internet, Herman Holtz, John Wiley & Sons.

Direct-Mail Books

Successful Direct Marketing Methods, Bob Stone, NTC Business Books.

Designing Direct Mail That Sells, Sandra Blum, North Light Books.

Publications

Consultants News, Templeton Rd., Fitzwilliam, NH 03447, (603) 585-2200.

Business Consultants Directory, American Business Directories Inc., 5711 S. 86th Cir., Omaha, NE 68127.

The Professional Consultant Newsletter, 123 NW Second, #405, Portland, OR 97209, (803) 224-2656.

Successful Consultants

The Barlett Group, Jeffery Barlett, 3690 Vartan Way, Harrisburg, PA 17110.

Melinda Patrician, 4229 S. 36th St., Arlington, VA 22206, (703) 824-1765.

Adhelp, Merrily Schiavone, 50 Millwright Dr., Newark, DE 19711, (302) 366-0681, fax: (302) 738-2642, <maschiavo@aol.com>.

LRS Marketing Inc., Roxanne Walker, 1915 E. Zabenko Dr., Wilmington, DE 19808, (302) 994-2147, fax: (302) 994-2147, <roxy1102@aol.com>.

Index